THROWING STRIKES

MY QUEST FOR TRUTH AND THE PERFECT KNUCKLEBALL

by R. A. Dickey

with

Wayne Coffey *and* Sue Corbett

DIAL BOOKS FOR YOUNG READERS

an imprint of Penguin Group (USA) Inc.

Table of Contents

Prologue

THE BEST SEASON OF MY LIFE

It is September 27, the day of my thirty-third start for the 2012 New York Mets. It has been another disappointing year for the team—a strong first half followed by a spirit-crushing collapse after the All-Star break. We're twenty-three games behind the Washington Nationals, too far back to contend for a wild card, even this year, when, for the first time, there are two spots.

It's a home game, our last of the season, but being home is not necessarily a plus. We have played miserably at Citi Field. Under the circumstances, it wouldn't be a surprise if the vendors outnumbered the spectators as we played out the string at this mid-week, afternoon game in late September.

Instead, there are thirty thousand people here. The press corps is out in force. And though I'm uncomfortable boasting, most of them are here because I am the starting pitcher. On the huge electronic marquee outside the stadium, there is only one announcement: R.A. GOES FOR 20 TODAY. It's so big, people on planes landing at LaGuardia Airport can see it from the air.

Twenty wins is the pinnacle for modern-day baseball pitchers. No Mets pitcher has won that many since Frank Viola went 20-12 in 1990.

Gio Gonzalez, the Nationals' young flamethrower, already has twenty wins, but no other pitcher in the National League has nineteen wins yet. At the moment, I lead the league in ERA, complete games, shutouts, and innings pitched. The baseball writers are predicting that Gio and I are the frontrunners for the Cy Young Award—given to the best pitcher in the National League. It's hard to get my mind around that.

In a month I will be thirty-eight years old, an age at which most of the guys I came up through the minors with have gotten used to being described with the word "former" in front of the words "major-league player."

Twenty wins in a season is a superlative effort for any pitcher, but for me, it's more than that. It's redemption. Before this year, I had won a *total* of forty-five games in the major leagues, despite having been a first-round draft pick, way back in 1996. Just two years ago, when I first started writing this book, I wrote these words and thoroughly believed them: "I will never lead the league in strikeouts."

As I take the mound to go for my twentieth win, I am leading the league in strikeouts.

It is seven years since my reinvention began. Six full seasons since I turned myself into the baseball equivalent of a carnival act—maybe not a two-headed turtle or a bearded lady, but close.

I became a knuckleballer.

You become a knuckleball pitcher when you hit a dead end, when your arm gets hurt or your fastball loses its velocity. Tim Wakefield was a minor-league first baseman with a lot of power but a weak batting average when he made the switch. I made mine when the Texas Rangers told me, in the middle of 2005, that I was going nowhere with my regular stuff—an assessment I could hardly argue with.

To say that I did not succeed immediately is understating things by quite a bit. In my debut as a knuckleballer, a 2006 game against the Detroit Tigers, I didn't make it out of the fourth inning, giving up seven runs on eight hits. Six of those hits were home runs, tying the modern record for most home runs given up in a start. That's a record nobody is chasing.

But six years later on this beautiful September day, as I walk in from the outfield with Josh Thole, who'll be catching me today, and Dan Warthen, the Mets' pitching coach, the fans in the seats just above the Mets' dugout rise to their feet.

I can honestly tell you I have never gotten a standing ovation *before* a start until today.

The first batter up for the Pirates is their rookie left fielder, Starling Marté. I strike him out on three straight pitches. All knucklers. I take the next batter, second baseman Josh Harrison, to a 2-2 count before he lines out to Andres Torres in center field. Then the dangerous Andrew McCutcheon, who is battling Buster Posey of the San Francisco Giants for the batting title and has as much at stake today as I do, flies out weakly to Ruben Tejada.

Twenty-four outs to go. I get another standing ovation as I head to the dugout. The crowd is chanting: *"Cy Young, Cy Young."* I keep my head down, trying to keep my focus.

How did I get from that epically horrible night in Arlington, Texas, to this incredible afternoon in Flushing Meadows? It took work, and not just work on mastering the fluttery delivery of the knuckler.

I had to overcome fear.

Fear that I wasn't good enough, that I didn't belong. Fear of people figuring that out. I have long had faith in God. What I had to find was faith in myself, and in the knuckleball.

The fact that I'm going for my twentieth win tells you I've turned it around. What it doesn't tell you is that it wasn't easy.

Chapter 1

LIFE BEGINS, ACCIDENTALLY

If you want to put it in baseball terms, you could say I was born with a strike against me. My parents didn't get married because they were hopelessly in love. They got married because my nineteen-year-old mother was pregnant with me.

It's not the ideal way to start a marriage, or a baby's life. Barely more than kids themselves, Harry and Leslie Dickey were still struggling to make ends meet, living in a part of Nashville crammed with pawnshops, used-car lots, and fast-food joints. The monthly rent for their apartment was $175 and they got what they paid for. The walls needed paint; cockroaches had their run of the place. Shortly after my parents scraped together enough money to move out, a particularly troublesome neighbor died—of a drug overdose.

We moved to 247 Timmons Avenue, to the house I think of as my first home. I remember the little wagon wheels on my red comforter, the school where I started kindergarten, and, unfortunately, the smoky haze that hung in my mother's beat-up Impala, a sorry heap with a gas tank that was always near empty.

I could give you a foot-by-foot description of my boyhood bedroom, highlighted by the Larry Bird photo I tore out of *Sports Illustrated* and taped to the wall. I have fond memories of my first glove, a twelve-dollar Kmart special, brown but definitely not leather. It was called the Mag. I still have no idea why. Maybe it was short for "Magician," or "Magnificent," or "Magadan," as in Dave, a former infielder for the New York Mets. I used the Mag when I played shortstop for Coach Teeter, my first Little League coach, who gave us yellow iron-on stars after we had a good game. I got my share of yellow stars, but they never made it onto my uniform. My mom had a lot going on.

My mother worked as a receptionist at a supply company. My father, Harry, a big man with broad shoulders, worked in construction during the day; at night, he was a security guard at the Davidson County Juvenile Delinquent Center.

My parents learned how to get by, but not how to get along. I hardly ever saw them hold hands or hug. The first two people I ever saw kiss were Luke Skywalker and Princess Leia in *Star Wars*.

Maybe my parents were too busy or too tired from work, or maybe they just didn't belong together. They stuck it out for as long as they could. People in my family are good at gritting things out. But when you fight a bunch and never kiss at all, grit is not enough. Their marriage barely lasted five years.

I spent my preschool years in Betty Waters's day-care center. My mom would pick me up after her shift, provided her car would start. There was only about a 50 percent chance it would start on any given day, but she got used to opening the hood and jiggling the wires in the distributor cap to get it going. On the way home one day, the car broke down about a half mile away from Betty's, so my mom left it on the shoulder, put me on her hip, and walked back to Betty's to call for help.

Halfway there, a German shepherd came running right at her, barking and baring its teeth. She kept walking, trying not to act scared, even though she was terrified. She shifted me to her left arm, away from the dog, which continued to growl. She hoped the dog would give up, but it didn't, sinking its teeth into her leg. She yelled and tried to shake free, but her mobility wasn't great with Baby Dickey in her arms. The dog got another couple of bites in. She yelled again and held me tight, telling herself over and over: Don't let it get my baby.

Finally, the dog retreated and my mom continued on her way to Betty's.

If you are a mother, you protect your children no matter what, my mother told me later. Nothing gets in the way of that.

My father, meanwhile, was confronted by choices. An A student who got his grades with minimal effort, he also drew favorable notices for his performances in his school's theater productions. Most of all, he excelled in both baseball and basketball, an athlete whom big-league scouts liked as a pitcher. Everybody called my father Horse. People said he could've had a professional baseball career, especially after impressive tryouts for the Cubs, the Reds, and the Cardinals. The Reds showed the most interest, offering him two thousand dollars and a bus ticket to Plant City, Florida, to join their minor-league team.

It was a dream opportunity, but it was also 1974, the year I was born, which eliminated that possibility. My father told the Reds he wanted to finish his education. "I can't see leaving school to go down to Plant City to see if I can be the one-in-a-thousand ballplayer who makes it to the big leagues," he said.

I don't know if the Reds tried to change his mind or if my father agonized over the decision. He never talked to me about his baseball dreams or about how he felt when the door on them closed. He never talked about how hard it was to be a young father, or about why he went from being a dad who would do everything with his son to a dad who more or less checked out. My heart still hurts over this because, by far, my favorite days in school were when the intercom would squawk in my classroom and somebody from the office would say: "Robert Dickey to the main office, please."

My dad would be waiting for me, having recorded some little lie in the sign-out book, like that I had a doctor's appointment, and off we'd go to Harpeth Hills Golf Course. He'd let me drive the cart and drink pop and knock the ball around. I wanted to play thirty-six holes.

Everything my dad and I did revolved around sports. We'd get two-dollar tickets for Nashville Sounds games, where I'd root for Don Mattingly, who later played first base in a much bigger stadium in the Bronx, New York. I'd chase foul balls all the way into the parking lot.

"Look what I got, Dad!" I'd say, showing the ball to my father.

"Way to go, Little Horsey," he'd respond. "Little Horsey" was his name for me.

I dreamed about playing in Herschel Greer Stadium one day, with my dad—the best ballplayer who ever lived—watching me. More than anything, I wanted a strong right arm like his. He could throw the highest high pops in the world. He'd fire them up in the sky and I'd wobble under them, hoping, somehow, the ball would land in my glove. When I won the beanbag toss competition at field day, I secretly credited my father with having given me his talent for pitching to a target.

My dad and I spent most of our free time together at the Green Hills Family YMCA, playing basketball. Although baseball was his best sport, my dad was a highly reliable shooting guard. He could bury outside shots all night, and his range was legendary. Twenty-five feet? Thirty feet? Horse would start looking at the basket just a few steps inside half-court. I loved watching him play, and watching him referee games when he started doing that to make a little extra cash.

Money was always an issue. I didn't go hungry, but finances were tight. I wore my uncle Ricky's hand-me-downs and if I absolutely needed something new, I'd get it at Kmart. We didn't go out to eat much, but if we did, it would be Western Sizzlin or someplace with a cheap buffet that let you load up your plate as often as you wanted. Western Sizzlin was where my parents got their first silverware. Not service for eight, just a few forks and knives and spoons they smuggled out.

After my parents split up, my younger sister, Jane, and I would sometimes visit our dad in his new place. It wasn't nice or big; there was no kitchen. It was kind of like camping out, minus the campfire. He'd make us macaroni and cheese on his hot plate. There was only room for one bed, so that's where the three of us slept.

Whatever we did and wherever we went, my father's advice to me was the same: Keep doing the work. You always have to do the work.

He never elaborated, but he liked saying those words. He liked language in general, liked the sound and texture of written and spoken English. He taught me one of my first grown-up vocabulary words: "enigma."

"You know what that means?" he asked. I didn't, of course.

"It means *mystery*. As in: 'He's always been an enigma to me.'"

My mom played sports too. She was a star shortstop in softball. Over the years, in fact, I wound up having a lot more catches with her than I did with my dad. I thought it was cool that my mom could make a play deep in the hole and gun a runner out, and that she'd slap a ball the other way, tear around the bases and hook-slide into home.

One team she played for was sponsored by Joe's Village Inn. She worked there as a cook, a waitress, and a bookkeeper, but was probably most valued for the way she fielded grounders. I'd go to her games, and then the whole team would head over to Joe's, a little roadside place that reeked of smoke and beer. Joe's was a friendly place. The people there were loud and happy. Sometimes very loud and ridiculously happy. I started going there when I was five, so the bartender, A.V., and I were on very good terms. He'd always give me a stack of quarters to spend on the games in the video arcade in the back.

My mother spent a lot of time at Joe's, and at Amber III, another Nashville bar with a softball team in need of a shortstop. The team would gather at one bar or another after games. Nobody wanted to leave, least of all my mother, whose teammates considered her the life of the party.

I got very good at Pac-Man.

Miller Lite was my mother's beverage of choice. It

surprised me how thirsty she got playing softball. A.V. kept filling up the pitchers of Miller Lite, and my mom and her teammates kept draining them. My mother acted silly herself after a while—a little loopy—and then we'd drive home in the beat-up Impala with an ashtray overflowing with cigarette butts.

As much as I liked playing Pac-Man, I recognized early on that Joe's Village Inn was a place Jane and I didn't belong. Of course we didn't belong there. Joe's was a bar and we were little kids.

Even at Joe's, though, my mom was always loving. The safest place in the world was in her lap. Her arms were always open for a hug. On the sofa at home, she would lie on her side with her legs bent at the knees and let me nestle into the triangular space between her heels and her hips. It was the best spot on earth to watch television.

We'd spend hours cuddled up that way, but slowly the Miller Lites began to intrude. The empties would pile up fast in the garbage. Sometimes my mom would fall asleep as soon as she got home. She was still loving, just not so available. She tried to keep up with how I was doing in school, but she wasn't much for helping with homework or getting to my games. She was a single mom who worked—and drank—hard.

With my dad already gone by the time I was in kindergarten, I learned to be by myself, and to seek diversions. I was good at that. I loved Luke Skywalker, because he was brave and ventured out in the world even though he didn't have a mother or father. I loved how Luke was his own person, and how boldly he lived. I even named my dog, a German shepherd–golden Lab mix, after him. The canine Luke and I spent a lot of time lying down in the front yard, with my head on his belly, in our own little world. If I wasn't there, I was with Lowell Dillon, my best pal. He lived right across from us on Timmons Street. Lowell and I were constantly playing football or war, the Cold War still enough of a vague threat that the object was always to get the Commies.

I'd eat Cap'n Crunch and watch the Braves on TBS, imitating Dale Murphy's deep crouch, the way the Braves' center fielder wiggled the bat back and forth. I'd retreat to my room and play with baseball cards or cut out photos from sports magazines and tape them to the wall. This was my gallery of heroes, my own Wall of Fame. I liked the safety of my room.

Other familiar places in my life felt less safe. I usually loved to visit the home of my mother's parents, whom I called MeeMaw and Granddaddy. They had a big yard on the crest of a hill, which was great for sledding when we were lucky enough to get snow.

The only trouble was you never knew what to expect from Granddaddy.

Granddaddy was the first knuckleball pitcher in the family. He fiddled around with it as a kid and got the hang of it, once using it to strike out sixteen batters in a six-inning game. He showed me a newspaper clipping to prove it.

But Granddaddy was like two different people. He loved to cook breakfast and dance around the kitchen with his apron on. He'd make me poached eggs and always keep fudge graham cookies in the refrigerator for me. That Granddaddy I loved beyond measure.

Granddaddy the whiskey drinker was a lot less lovable. When he got to his second or third glass, he'd get ornery. He'd start yelling at MeeMaw and could be real hard on his seven kids, my mom and her twin sister, Lynn, being two of them.

One Christmas, the year I was nine, Granddaddy lit into MeeMaw over something silly. Uncle Ricky, the youngest of the seven, had had enough.

Uncle Ricky was one of my heroes, maybe the best athlete in the family, an uber-competitive guy who was a five-foot-nine-inch All-American basketball player at Lipscomb University and one of the hardest-hitting

150-pound safeties in the annals of Nashville prep football. If you were playing a game or going into battle, Ricky Bowers was the guy you wanted on your side. And the guy you least wanted to see on the other side.

"Daddy, knock it off," Uncle Ricky told him.

"You don't tell me what I can or can't say in my house," Granddaddy said. He cussed at Uncle Ricky, who cussed back, and then it was on, a full-blown fistfight.

I couldn't bear to look anymore. These were two of the people I loved the most in the whole world. I didn't want them to fight. I couldn't stop it. I didn't want to be there at all.

My mom and sister and I went back home to Timmons Street. Nobody said much. I didn't know what went on in other families. I didn't know what normal was. I just knew what I saw that day made me scared of my own family.

I blamed alcohol. All it did was cause problems. I'd seen fights at Joe's Village Inn and the Amber III, seen people slurring and stumbling. I'd watched alcohol turn good, gentle people into monsters.

I made a promise to myself then and there: I would never drink alcohol. Never.

Chapter 2

FOUR YEARS, FOUR SCHOOLS

I f only I could have also pledged to refrain from fist-fights.

Fights were not an everyday occurrence in my neighborhood, but I single-handedly did what I could to bring the average up. I fought to defend myself, to right a wrong, or to settle a dispute. I wasn't picky. I might as well have worn one of those sandwich-board signs with the message DON'T MESS WITH ME on it.

There was a reason for this. But it was a reason I refused to share with anyone. Not for a couple of decades.

I didn't worry about pain or getting knocked down. I just got back up and hurled myself at my opponent like a boomerang. My goal was to give more than I received. I wasn't proud of this; I thought what I was doing was about survival.

I trained myself to act tough when I needed to, and

sometimes when I didn't need to, which got me into trouble. One day in seventh grade, I got up from my assigned seat in the lunchroom because I needed the homework assignment from a classmate. A monitor barked at me to get back to my seat.

He was nasty about it. I decided I didn't like his tone and cussed under my breath. Not loud, not even a bad cussword, but an audible obscenity, no doubt.

Now he didn't like my tone.

"Come with me, young man," he commanded. "You are going to regret your garbage mouth."

He was right: I did regret it—because in Tennessee in the 1980s, corporal punishment still ruled the day. The monitor took me to see Mr. Timmon, the assistant principal, who conveniently kept the paddle right next to his desk.

"Bend over," he ordered, walloping me on the butt three times before suspending me for three days.

Three days? For one whispered cussword? I didn't think the punishment fit the crime, but no one asked for my opinion. I served my sentence, but whether I learned any lesson from it was less clear. I had my first fight in seventh grade two weeks later, against a big kid whose name I never learned. I don't remember how or why we wound up in the school parking lot, but there we were, a couple of dopes with our dukes up, ready to rumble.

My usual strategy was to barge right in and see what the guy had, watching especially to see if he closed his eyes when he threw a punch. Most kids did. And when they did, they gave me an opening to end things quickly. This kid hit me with a few minor punches, closing his eyes with every jab. I stepped back as he cocked his arm to throw another one and ripped an uppercut into his jawbone. Blood spurted out of a gash in his face and he went down. Hard.

I looked at him, lying there in a bloody heap, and at my blood-splattered right knuckle. Then I picked up my stuff and headed for home as casually as if we'd met for afternoon tea. I returned to my empty house, had a bowl of Froot Loops, and climbed the poplar tree in the front yard. I wondered if the kid was still laid out in the parking lot. I couldn't believe how little I cared.

I never mentioned the fight to anybody.

The next time I fought, I used the same full-bore approach. We were playing football near my house, and this older kid, strong and sinewy, took me down with a vicious tackle.

"What do you think you're doing?" I said, scrambling to my feet.

"What's your problem, punk? Can't take a hit?"

We squared off and before I could even figure out if he closed his eyes when he punched people, he drove a fist into my temple and knocked me to the ground, finishing the job by kicking me in the gut with what felt like a steel-toed boot. TKO in the first round. The other kids dispersed. This time I was the one left on the ground. Some boomerang.

A stray dog came over to sniff me. I slowly got to my feet, mad at myself that I couldn't take the kid's punch, furious at him that he used a kick to end it.

I never mentioned this fight to anybody either.

In the span of four years, I switched from Glencliff Elementary to St. Edward School to Wright Middle School. Whatever my address, I continued to find my way into tangles and had a strange lack of concern about pain. Actually, I didn't care about lots of things.

My parents, both of them, were concerned. Uncle Ricky was worried about me too. The consensus was that I, like Uncle Ricky, should enroll at Montgomery Bell Academy, a prestigious, all-boys school in one of Nashville's nicest neighborhoods. Uncle Ricky went to school there on an athletic scholarship and set all sorts of school records in baseball and basketball. It changed his life.

I took the rigorous entrance exam. And failed it. Maybe because I didn't really care about that, either. I didn't take it seriously enough. The night before the test, I played in a basketball tournament. Maybe I should have done some prep work for the test instead.

Whatever the reason, I felt overmatched. The sense of disappointment among my family was impossible to miss. Even I felt disappointment. Deep down, I think I knew I needed a big intervention. I needed something to change the direction of my life, a life that, as much as I wanted to deny it, to hide it, to run away from the truth, started to go off the skids the summer I was eight years old, when a series of bad things happened to me. They were really bad, ugly things. My response was to bottle up a secret so toxic, it was poisoning me, changing me into somebody I didn't want to be. I should've talked to somebody about it, I know that now. But I didn't, because I was scared and ashamed and afraid that I had done something terribly wrong.

So I went back to Wright Middle School to finish seventh grade, with my secret still jammed as far back in my brain as it would go. I became good at compartmentalizing things, boxing them away into secret places forever.

Much better that they stay boxed away forever. Things are safe in boxes.

I never told anyone my terrible secret until I was thirty-one years old.

Chapter 3

STARTING OVER

I took the MBA entrance exam again and this time, I passed it. Largely on the strength of Uncle Ricky's athletic legacy, the school offered me a full package of financial aid. If I was willing to—gulp—repeat seventh grade, I was in. I agreed to repeat seventh grade.

Montgomery Bell Academy was founded in 1867 and ever since has been educating Nashville's elite, an income group I knew nothing about. Many MBA students have parents who will leave them generous inheritances. I had parents who smuggled flatware from Western Sizzlin. I wasn't the only kid from the other side of the proverbial tracks, but I was in the minority, for sure.

By the time I hit my new, hoity-toity hallways, almost everybody was calling me R.A. It stands for Robert Allen. I was Robert for most of my life, but people in the family called my grandfather R.G., for Robert Green, and they shortened my name to my initials too. The only person who continued to call me Robert was my mother, though it's lucky she wasn't calling me much worse.

I was giving my mother a hard time about everything. Cleaning my room, hanging up my coat, taking out the trash—I battled her over the most mundane chores, and found new ways, daily, to be defiant. As the time to start at MBA approached, I went for the jugular.

"I'm going to go live with Dad," I announced. I didn't ask permission.

She couldn't have been more stunned if I'd told her I was quitting sports to take up the cello. "What's wrong with living here?"

"Nothing, I just want to live with Dad."

She reminded me that she had custody; it was not my choice, but I'd already left the room. I don't know why my mother didn't just bring down the hammer and tell me I wasn't going anywhere. My mother was still holding down a job, but her drinking had gotten worse. Deep down, I knew she was ashamed about the way her life had turned out. She probably didn't feel entitled to stand up for herself.

A couple of weeks later, moving day arrived. I headed downstairs with my duffel bag when I heard my father's car pull up. My mother was in her blue recliner. I didn't hug or kiss her or thank her for everything she'd done over the first twelve years of my life. I behaved, quite honestly, like a completely self-involved punk. I just walked out the door and got into my father's car. The last sound I heard leaving 247 Timmons was my mother sobbing; big, heaving, gasping-for-air kind of sobs. I could hear her all the way out to my dad's car.

It was bravado, but I convinced myself my mother's tears didn't bother me. I was a child of divorce learning how to numb myself to pain, whether it came from other kids' punches, or from the damage I inflicted on others, even people I loved.

The whole point of this power play was to get close to my dad again. It wasn't about getting away from my mother's drinking or about the towels she wanted me to pick up. It wasn't about having more independence. It was driven entirely by this yearning to be back at the Green Hills YMCA, or chasing foul balls at Sounds games, or driving a golf cart with my father next to me, both of us hoping to play thirty-six holes.

That's what I wanted. More than anything else, I wanted to hear my dad call me Little Horsey and have everything be the way it was before he left, before the divorce and all the instability, before the summer I was eight years old.

It'll be great, Dad, don't you think? That's what I wanted to say to my father, but I never worked up my nerve to get the words out.

There wasn't any part of Montgomery Bell Academy that didn't intimidate me at first. I didn't know the buildings, the teachers, or even where the bathrooms were. My classmates wore Ralph Lauren Polo shirts, with the logo of a man on a horse with a polo mallet. I wore knock-off Knights of the Round Table shirts, with a less familiar logo of a man on a horse with a flag. Nobody mocked me for my clothes, but I was aware of moving in a whole different orbit. I'd never heard of a school having a motto ("Gentleman, Scholar, Athlete"), and I'd never had to adhere to an academic honor code, either. Every time I submitted an assignment or took a test, I wrote these words and signed my name beneath them: "On my honor as a gentleman, I have neither given nor received aid on this work."

The biggest difference was the splendor of the place itself: columned brick buildings with wide porches, and old stone walls that seem to go on forever. In the main courtyard are two Civil War cannons. Not models of Civil War cannons. *Real* Civil War cannons.

I felt like a Wookiee at a White House dinner, but I was determined to fit in because there were things I really liked about MBA too. I liked the order and the discipline. I may have complained about the rules, but privately I relished them. Most of all, people paid attention to me and seemed genuinely interested in helping me. That didn't happen in all that many places. I knew my mother loved me, but she had her own problems. My dad had remarried by that point, and my stepmother, Susan, was awfully nice to me, driving me all over Nashville to practices and games, but she was not my mother (and self-absorbed punk that I was, I never let her forget that). At home, I mostly felt alone. I didn't feel quite so alone at MBA.

As the first days of the seventh grade turned into weeks, I met an eighth grader named Bo Bartholomew. I didn't make friends easily, feeling far more comfortable sitting in the back, observing, calculating and measuring my options. I had a hard time trusting anyone. I was a kid who had secrets, and was terrified that those secrets would somehow be uncovered.

But something about Bo felt safe. He played on the school football team with me. Looking at his muscles made me hope that MBA kids didn't fight the way we did on the other side of town. Smart and strong and handsome, Bo looked as if he stepped right out of a J.Crew catalog.

But Bo turned out to be very different from other kids I'd been around. Kind, generous, and concerned about other people, he treated me as a complete equal. He invited me to his house in Belle Meade, the swankiest neighborhood in Nashville, where I met his mother, Vicki Bartholomew. She had been Miss Tennessee in 1966, second runner-up to Miss America, and twenty-two years later she was still a beautiful woman with a welcoming spirit. She offered us a snack before we headed upstairs to play Duck Hunt on Bo's Nintendo. I had never seen a Nintendo. We played for an hour before deciding to go out to throw the football. As we turned the corner into the den to head outside, I stopped still.

On the couch, curled up with her homework, was Bo's younger sister, Anne, a green-eyed beauty with wavy blond hair so thick, it looked like a lion's mane.

Bo introduced me.

"Nice to meet you," said Anne, who was also in seventh grade, but at a different private school.

"You too," I answered. The words had barely escaped when I wanted them back. *That's the best you can do? You too?*

Bo and I wanted to toss the football, but all I could think about was Anne and how I probably sounded like a caveman to her.

Hanging out in school the next day, I wanted to talk to Bo about his sister, but he wanted to talk about a meeting for a group called the Fellowship of Christian Athletes. He wanted me to come with him.

I played three sports—football, basketball, and baseball—so the word "athletes" was a hook. "What is it?" I asked.

"It's a fellowship of guys who get together to share about their faith in God," Bo said.

I didn't know much about God. I'd only been to church a few times, with my grandmother. I had some big doubts about attending the meeting, but I told Bo I'd go, mostly because I was really interested in his sister.

I arrived early. I had a good bit of courage as I entered the room, but it faded with every new face that came through the door. There were at least thirty boys.

What would I do if they asked me to pray or to share about myself? Would they throw me out for being an impostor? Under my jacket, it felt like I'd just stepped out of the swimming pool, that's how much I was sweating. Was getting to know Bo's sister really worth all this?

The meeting opened with a prayer and then guys talked about their lives and their struggles and how a relationship with God gave them peace and stability. I found myself drawn to those words. Peace and stability. They sounded like something I wanted.

Nobody made me testify to anything or put me on the spot. I went back to more meetings, and began to get a greater sense of what a relationship with God meant to other people in the room, and to Bo. There really did seem to be a difference in the way they treated people, and the way they dealt with adversity, owning up to their mistakes and not looking around for someone to blame.

One Friday, Bo invited me to spend the night at his house. I eagerly accepted (hoping, of course, to see Anne again). But I had some questions I wanted to ask Bo, about becoming a Christian. "How do you do it?" I wondered. "Where do you start?"

"When you feel you are ready, you just invite Him into your life," Bo said.

I heard Mrs. Bartholomew coming up the stairs. She'd overheard Bo's answer to my question and joined us. I was uneasy, because I didn't know her very well yet, but when she and Bo finished talking, I knew I wanted to try to have what they had: a relationship with God.

This was uncharted territory for me. Over the past few weeks, I had heard words that spoke to my core, but that I had no personal connection with: "Peace." "Stability." "Forgiveness." They sounded good, but they seemed totally beyond me, like trying to hold the ocean in two cupped hands. How was I supposed to do that?

But I was determined to try. So on a fall Friday in an upstairs bedroom on Walnut Drive in Nashville, Tennessee, I got on my knees with Bo and his mom. I clasped my hands clumsily and blurted it out: *I want a relationship with Jesus Christ.* I said that I believed He was the son of God, and that I trusted Him with my life. Secretly, I asked for forgiveness for what seemed like a galaxy of sins and guilt and shame.

When I finished speaking, the room was completely still. I felt relief, a lightness. It wasn't the sky opening up, or angels singing, or lightning bolts striking the big magnolia in the front yard. Nothing like that. It was subtle, like the best deep breath you could ever take. I had instantly found comfort putting my fate in the hands of a God who loved me, secrets and all.

Why I Pray

Since that afternoon on Walnut Drive, prayer has become a part of my daily life. To me, prayer is not something I turn to only when I have a personal crisis, and especially not something I rely on when I'm hoping to pitch a dominant game. I've never asked God, "Lord, please let me strike out Albert Pujols four times tonight." Nor will I ever do that. God is not a genie in a bottle that you rub when you want something. Prayer is how I deepen my relationship with God, and how I try to understand His plan for me. Throughout my career, prayer is how I reminded myself that if I didn't succeed as a big-league pitcher, it was because God had something else in store for me, and whatever that was, I would be at peace.

Chapter 4

RISKY BUSINESS

Though my soul was still very much a work-in-progress, my skills on the playing fields at school were earning me a reputation. I played football and basketball for MBA, but it was clear early on that baseball was the sport where I could excel.

The first man to impress that upon me was Fred Forehand. His name suggests he should have taken up tennis, but he was MBA's baseball coach. Coach Forehand was a small guy with a larger-than-life personality. I'm not sure I ever saw him dressed in anything other than a maroon-and-white MBA sweat suit. In the winter of my eighth-grade year, Coach Forehand told me he expected me to try out for the varsity squad. "You've got a chance to be our shortstop," he said.

Starting shortstop for a really good high school baseball team? In eighth grade? I couldn't believe Coach Forehand thought that much of me. It was empowering. I may have had my secrets, and I'd gotten good at not letting anybody get too close to me. But now I embraced an identity: I was an athlete. You couldn't be in the running for the MBA shortstop in eighth grade if you weren't an athlete.

The competition for the starting job came down to a freshman named Brett Miller and me, on the last day before our games began. Coach Forehand had a fungo bat and he was running a situational drill—runner on first and two out. He smacked a grounder in the hole between third and short. It rolled up the third baseman's arm and bounced off his shoulder. I was behind him and caught the ball off his shoulder, deep in the hole. I gunned the ball to first.

My throw beat the runner by a half step.

The next day I became the starting shortstop, and I stayed there for five years, except when I pitched.

Life in the classroom was not as smooth as on the infield. A big issue for me was demerits. You got demerits if your shirttail was out or you were late for class or you missed an assignment. When a teacher spotted an infraction, he or she called you on it and you earned demerits on the spot. I racked up demerits the way Mariano Rivera racked up saves. I led the school in them, getting fifty in one year alone, most because of my unruly shirttail.

Every demerit earned me a half hour in Saturday school. My weekends got pretty tied up.

Discipline was not my greatest strength as a student, either, especially in English. I didn't like to bother with punctuation or spelling or grammar, which explained why I routinely got papers handed back to me that looked like they were bleeding. I did care about stories. I loved telling stories, but the fine points of grammar? Boring. I was king of the run-on sentences that slithered snakelike, were overly ambitious, and tried to do too much by being excruciatingly overwritten and practically leaving the reader gasping for air, waiting breathlessly for the period to arrive.

Phew.

Miss Brewer tried to rein me in. She was one of my English teachers, and, startlingly, thought I had some ability with language. Her calm voice flowed like the long skirts she wore, and she was nurturing, always encouraging students to take on new challenges. One day, she called me over after class.

"R.A., there's a regional poetry contest coming up and I'd love to see you enter it. I think you have a gift," she said.

"Thanks, Miss Brewer, but I have written a total of

about four poems in my life," I told her. "I don't want to embarrass myself."

"Oh, trust me, you won't," she insisted. "You have an original mind and an appreciation of language. Being creative is all about taking risks, anyway. Why not try?"

I grudgingly agreed to write a couple of poems, and Miss Brewer submitted them to the competition. One of the poems was written in traditional iambic pentameter—you know, Shakespeare's style—the other was a haiku. I actually enjoyed writing them, but I didn't tell her that.

A few weeks later, we gathered in the auditorium to hear the results of the competition. The master of ceremonies announced: "The winner of the poetry contest is . . . R. A. Dickey."

I was sure there had been a mistake. Was I the only one who entered? I walked up to the stage, flabbergasted, and shook the emcee's hand, more sheepish than proud. Miss Brewer, who was thrilled, told me later I won the competition for my haiku:

Lifelike buttercups
Sway in graceful unison
With the midnight breeze

Tommy Owen wasn't big on nurturing, but what do you expect? He was the football coach and he was one tough guy. His body was as taut as a cable, his voice deep and raspy—though he didn't use it much when he was really angry. He preferred just to bore a hole through you with his stare.

Everybody in school called him Coach Owen, even in the classroom, where he taught history, his principal topic being World War II—a subject he had firsthand knowledge of because he served as a navigator on a B-24 Liberator. Coach Owen taught me about the Luftwaffe, Hitler's propaganda machine, and the Normandy invasion. Then, after school, we'd head out to the football field, where the lessons switched to post patterns and play-action passes. I was the quarterback, and I had a lot to learn.

Of all the things Coach Owen loathed on the football field, lack of discipline and mental mistakes topped the list. I accomplished both in a single play against Hillwood High one Friday night, dropping back to pass at their twenty-five yard line as Hillwood blitzed. I scrambled, retreating and dodging and retreating some more, channeling my inner Brett Favre. I was all the way back at midfield, trying to keep the play alive, when I heard

Coach Owen hollering, "Throw it out of bounds!" I kept scrambling and he kept hollering, but I finally saw an opening and started going forward, running left. At the forty yard line, I picked out a receiver, Mark Fuqua, in the clear near the end zone. I threw the ball all the way across the field. It traveled in an ugly wobble, but Mark grabbed it and scored the game-winning touchdown. We began our celebration, which ended the moment I got to the sideline.

Coach Owen grabbed my face mask to snap my head toward him. His face was an inch or two away from the bars of my helmet. It was in full-bore glare mode.

"When I tell you to throw the ball out of bounds, son, you throw the ball out of bounds," he said.

He sounds intense, but Coach Owen helped me grow up by not going in for hand-holding. We beat a tough team from inner-city Nashville, Pearl-Cohn Comprehensive High School, one time, and were heading back to our bus. I had my helmet off, walking alongside Eric Crawford, our fullback, when a gang of kids ambushed us. Eric got slugged in the side of the face and fell hard. Just as I tried to help him up, I felt something smash into the back of my head. I dropped to a knee. I turned to see our assailants running away. On the ground next to me was their weapon, a brown bottle that somehow did not break on impact with my skull.

The coaches hurried us onto the bus without further incident. But as we pulled away, Coach Owen walked back to my seat and gave me the glare again.

"That's why you always keep your helmet on," he said, and then returned to the front of the bus.

R.A.'S TIPS FOR YOUNG PITCHERS

Play more than one sport. *I played basketball, baseball, and football in junior high and high school. The lessons I learned in the other sports made me a better baseball player, and they were lessons I could only have learned on the court or on the football field. Working with more than one coach helped me develop, because every coach has a different method of motivation. You never know when you might hear something that makes it all "click." Playing the same sport all year long also puts a lot of strain on the same set of muscles. We live in a culture now that believes that the only way to move up the athletic ladder is to specialize in a single sport, but there's a downside to that if your body never gets a chance to rest, repair, and replenish itself.*

While I was learning to navigate my way (and keep my shirttail tucked in) at MBA, my mother graduated from beer to vodka. Once I decided to live with my father, it all began to pile up for her, like cars in a NASCAR wreck. She thought she'd failed as a mother, starting with the times she hauled my sister and me with her to Joe's Village Inn and Amber III. My mom was in pain, and the time-honored way to medicate pain in her family was to drink.

But I was so occupied with sports and my new life that I didn't pay much attention to my mother's problems. The more I immersed myself in MBA's athletic culture, the more it insulated me from my mother's alcoholism and my father's increasing remoteness. I put my trust in baseball and football and basketball; in my ability to play and the knowledge that the games would be played by a particular set of rules, even if you didn't win. I did not have the same trust in my own mother and father. My relationship with my mother became distant. My father became a man I couldn't figure out. I was never even sure if he came to my football games. I'd think I saw him in the stands, but he never hung around afterward. I never got to ask him how I played, or what advice he had, or to celebrate with him. When my friends' parents took them out for dinner or dessert, I was the tagalong.

Sports never checked out on me. There was always another game, another season. Game days and game nights were the best times of my life. The ball fields and gyms of Montgomery Bell Academy became my sanctuary.

My mother finally realized she couldn't continue on the course she was on and checked herself into a rehabilitation facility for a thirty-day treatment program. She'd been there two weeks already before I worked up the courage to go see her.

I walked into the main building, my anxiety growing. I wanted my mother to get the help she needed, but I was apprehensive about the whole visit, a feeling heightened when I got a whiff of that antiseptic hospital smell. I wondered whether my mom would be escorted out by two guys in white jackets.

I waited in a large room with tables and chairs, and ashtrays every three feet, all of them spilling over with cigarette butts. After a few minutes, my mother arrived with an orderly. She looked . . . healthier. Her eyes were clear. We walked around a pond, and she told me how she was facing hard truths about her own family background and learning to take responsibility for her behavior. Back then, I didn't fully grasp the concept of alcoholism being a disease or the challenges of recovery, but I saw a difference in my mother already.

What would she be like when she got out, I wondered. Would she be someone I could fully trust again? I wasn't sure. But I hugged her and told her that I loved her. As I drove out of the stone gate, my guard was a little bit lower than it was when I drove in.

Late one Friday night in my junior year, after an MBA victory, we went to our usual postgame hangout for food and high-quality milk shakes. When we finished, it was almost eleven o'clock. We had practice first thing in the morning. My dad's house was twenty minutes away, across town.

I didn't feel like making the trip, knowing I had to be back at school first thing. Often I crashed with friends who lived right in Green Hills, kids like David Fitzgerald or Tiger Harris or Mike Anderson, my catcher in baseball, but I worried about wearing out my welcome. But I was also sure I didn't want to go home. Home didn't feel like home. It was where my father and stepmother lived, but it wasn't a place where I felt safe and comfortable. It was just four walls and a roof.

I'm not saying it was my dad's fault. Maybe it was mine. It just didn't feel like I belonged there. The feeling of family was missing. We didn't have many meals together, or play board games together, or do much of anything together. My father seemed to be there in body only, as if he had something much bigger on his mind. I didn't know what that something was. An enigma? Yes, that's what he was to me. An enigma. There were no rules or discipline, no curfews or consequences. I just came and went as I pleased. I was a kid crying out for limits, and getting none.

"The nomad checks back in," my father once remarked, when I showed up after a few nights away. He didn't ask where I'd been or what I'd been up to. I could've been stealing cars or dealing drugs, for all he knew. I wanted to believe my dad was proud of me and that he loved me, but he shared his thoughts and opinions very rarely. It wasn't even that I was angry that he didn't. It was more that I missed him. I wanted him to be the most important man in my life.

Can you do that for me, Dad? I wanted to ask, but I never did.

More and more, I spent my time at the Bartholomews' or with my aunt and uncle Billy and Lynn Caldwell, whose doors and hearts were always open. This was what I craved. I wanted to be in a place where hearts were open. I wanted to sit around the dinner table and listen to people talk about their day and share their feelings and concerns. I wanted to pray together as a family.

So that night I drove around Green Hills, instead of driving home. I could sleep in my car, I told myself. No, I wouldn't get any sleep. I had a sweatshirt and a couple of towels in the backseat. What about sleeping outside, on the golf course? Nah, I was not a sleep-under-the-stars kind of guy, and besides, the grounds guys started mowing and raking sand traps at five in the morning.

All through Green Hill this went on. I kept driving, thinking, *What am I going to do?* On a lawn, I saw a sign: FOR RENT. I pulled over. It was a brick home with a nice fenced yard. The house was dark and appeared empty.

Dueling voices fired up in my head.

VOICE ONE: Maybe you can stay here tonight. You won't damage anything. You'll sleep and leave. No harm, no foul.

VOICE TWO: You can't break into somebody's house and sleep in it. Are you out of your mind? That's a crime.

VOICE ONE: It'll be an adventure. It's just one night.

VOICE TWO: It's insanity. You are not doing this.

I parked up the road a bit and walked back to the house to do some reconnaissance, peering through the windows. I didn't see an alarm or a dog or furniture. The house was vacant. I decided that if I could find a key, this was where I would spend the night.

Voice One drowned out Voice Two.

Now I had to find the key. Real estate agents aren't that imaginative when it comes to hiding keys. I poked around out front, but no luck. I contemplated breaking a window, but my lawlessness had limits. I went around to the back of the house. There was a single pot on the back porch containing a half-dead fern. Under the pot I found a key. I felt like Bilbo Baggins in the Misty Mountains when he stumbles on the Ring of Power. I put the key in the lock and, after a quarter turn to the right, I was in.

I walked into the darkness, tiptoeing. I was in the kitchen, I think. My heart throbbed and I realized I would be a terrible criminal. I moved slowly into different rooms to confirm the house was empty. Voice Two resurfaced.

What if you are arrested and MBA finds out? What will happen? You'll be a goner from MBA, that's what'll happen. This is reckless, stupid. There is still time to get out before trouble arrives.

All valid points. I ignored them: This was where I was spending the night.

From the car I grabbed my sweatshirt and towels, the extent of my supplies. I laid the towels down in a corner of the bare living room floor and built a terry-cloth bed. I put on my sweatshirt, lay down, and looked at the water stains on the ceiling.

They may want to check that out, I thought. It could explain why the house hasn't attracted any tenants.

My heart settled down. I fell asleep quickly.

The next morning, I gathered my towels and made my way out the back door as if it were my own house. I locked up and replaced the key under the dead fern. I headed to football practice.

I slept in vacant houses another half-dozen times over the next two years, and became a practiced vacant house scout. On nights when I thought it might be a possibility, I went to the library to look in the classifieds for homes close to school, on quiet streets with ample parking. I kept a sleeping bag and pillow in the trunk of my car at all times, just in case. It got easier, breaking into other people's houses. I enjoyed the hunt for the key, the rush of being somewhere I wasn't supposed to be. I don't know why. Other than speed limits, I had never broken a law. I liked the danger, the independence, and maybe, most of all, the power to choose. I was still lonely, but it was a loneliness of my own choosing.

WHAT I BELIEVE

Why I Write

I started keeping a journal when I was fourteen, jotting down anecdotes about things that happened each day. But I quickly wanted to do more than just record facts. I needed to make sense of them.

Writing allowed me, in small, private doses, to think about which things mattered to me and how those things fit into the larger story that was my life. Later on, writing became a way of sharing something with my family when I had to be away, or communicating a message about the things I think are important in a speech.

Well-chosen words can have an impact and a permanence that a phone call or a text message will never have. There's not much in this world that has more endurance than a well-told story.

Every day, each of us is creating our own story. Every day, a new page is written. Only you can tell your story. The way to figure out what your story is, is to start writing it down.

Chapter 5

MAGNIFICENT

By my senior year at MBA, I had stayed at a lot of different houses, both occupied and vacant, and played a ton of ball games, as a quarterback, shooting guard, and pitcher/shortstop. Some Division II and Division III schools had dangled scholarships for football and basketball, but my desire to play baseball had solidified. Credit for that had to be given to Coach Forehand.

Through good games and bad, Coach Forehand was there for me, a kind and fatherly constant. I spent so much time following him around, asking him questions, he nicknamed me Lapdog, which my teammates happily adopted as their own name for me. I guess it would be fair to say I was the coach's pet, in a way. One year, the day the uniforms arrived, Coach whispered to me in an almost conspiratorial voice: "Go pick out the one you want, Lapdog, before the troops arrive."

Coach Forehand did thoughtful little things like that for me ever since we'd met. I'd just started playing for him when he motioned for me to meet him on the side of the field. I ran in from shortstop, with the Mag, my twelve-dollar Kmart glove I'd been using since I started playing Little League. I never did a survey, but I'm sure the Mag was the oldest and worst glove on the team.

"Just in case you are thinking about getting a new glove," Coach Forehand said, "Poe's Sporting Goods is a good place to go. Mr. Poe has real nice gloves and he's a friend of MBA and he'll give you a good deal."

Since money was tight, as usual, I had not really been thinking about getting a new glove, but I took Coach Forehand's comment to mean he thought it was time for an upgrade. I told Granddaddy about it and he agreed to take me to Poe's.

Poe's had a whole wall of beautiful gloves. The place smelled like leather. I could've stayed there all day. I tried out a few gloves before coming upon a Wilson A2000. It was black, with a beautiful, deep pocket, the nicest glove I'd ever seen. I wanted it desperately, so I looked for the price tag.

Oh, jeez. One hundred dollars. No way we could afford a one-hundred-dollar glove.

I put the glove back as Mr. Poe ambled over. "That A2000 is a beauty, isn't it?" he asked.

I agreed but had to tell him it was out of my price range.

He pulled the glove off the shelf and put it back in my hands. I wasn't sure what he was doing; I had just finished telling him we couldn't spend that much.

"The cost of the glove has been taken care of, young man," Mr. Poe said. "Now go play some ball with it."

"Excuse me, what did you say?" I asked.

"The glove is yours. It's all squared away," he said.

Squared away, as in mine? To keep? I couldn't even take it in. Somebody just bought me the best glove in the world? Was this for real? I thanked Mr. Poe again and again and shook his hand, and left the store with the A2000 on my hand.

Years later I found out that Granddaddy and Mr. Poe were in cahoots with Coach Forehand to get me a new glove. Coach had seen enough of the Mag, that's for sure.

Midway through my senior year, 1993, Jeff Forehand, Fred's son, pulled me aside for a talk. Jeff, a former second baseman for nearby Belmont University, was an assistant coach for MBA. "I don't know how to put this, but we just found out my dad has cancer, and it's at a pretty advanced stage," he said. "He doesn't want to make a big deal out of it and doesn't even want to tell the team, but I wanted you to know."

There weren't words for how sad this made me, but I fumbled out some remarks to try to convey how sorry I was.

"He's starting chemo right away," Jeff told me. "We just have to hope and pray for the best."

R.A.'S TIPS FOR YOUNG PITCHERS

Be coachable. *Athletes who are unwilling to listen to what coaches have to teach them are athletes who will often find themselves sitting on the bench. It's all right to not have all the answers.*

I promised Jeff that his dad, my coach, would be in every prayer I recited.

Coach Forehand kept right on teaching and coaching as he underwent treatment. But by the time our season got under way, he looked gaunt. Everybody on the team knew what was going on, but Coach never talked about it, and definitely never complained. He just kept directing drills and hitting fungoes to get us ready to play, doing it all with a colostomy bag attached to his abdomen.

We won our district and regional titles and made it all the way to the state championship game, against Germantown at Middle Tennessee State University. Coach Forehand looked thin and weak. The months of treatment had taken a huge toll, but he was determined to keep going and so were his players. Over three days, I pitched twenty-one innings and gave up one run. The title came down to a single final game. I entered the game in relief in the fifth with the score tied, 1–1. It stayed tied into the ninth. With pinch runner Ted Morrissey on second, Trent Batey, our shortstop, lined a shot over the Germantown left fielder's head and within moments, we were all in a pile on the field, hugging Ted and Trent and anybody else we could find. It was bedlam, a tangle of maroon-and-white uniforms everywhere you looked, and right in the middle of it, all I could see was Coach Forehand. He had a smile on his face and the game ball in his hand. A single tear trailed down his right cheek. I walked over to him. Now I had a tear running down my cheek. I hugged him for a long time, and said the only thing I could think of:

I love you, Coach.

Chapter 6

VOLUNTEERING FOR DUTY

In the fall of 1993, I arrived at Gibbs Hall, the athletic dormitory at the University of Tennessee, with two duffel bags of sweatshirts and sweatpants, and the mind-set of a walk-on. I was a top recruit, I guess, but I wasn't fond of the recruiting process, which is basically Smoke Blowing 101. Everybody tells you how great you are and they have pretty girls escort you around campus and introduce some players, who want to take you out for a night on the town, as if this were all part of a typical day.

I didn't want to be fussed over or go out on the town. I just wanted to take some interesting English classes and play baseball at the highest level possible. I wasn't there long before I got a glimpse of somebody able to play at that level, with ease: Todd Helton.

Helton was recruited to play football and baseball at Tennessee. He was the backup quarterback to Heath

Shuler in his first two years, and then as a junior was the backup to Jerry Colquitt, who had waited years himself to get a chance to play. In the season opener, Colquitt tore ligaments in his knee; Helton took over. Three weeks later, Helton banged up his own knee and got replaced by some kid named Peyton Manning.

Helton knew his future was in baseball, and after people saw Manning play, he wasn't getting the job back anyway. Helton eventually quit football, but in the fall of my freshman year, he was still playing. We were having a baseball workout one day when Helton showed up during a break in football practice, wearing his orange jersey and cleats.

"Can I jump in and get a couple of swings?" Helton asked. He grabbed a wooden bat. On his second swing, he crushed a ball far over the right-field fence.

"That's good, thanks," he said, before heading back to football practice. I tried not to stare.

Helton is one of the greatest clutch hitters I've ever seen. During the NCAA regionals my freshman year, we were down by four runs in the eighth inning against Arizona State when he came up with the bases loaded. One swing later, the game was tied. Helton came through again and again with his bat, but he was also a phenomenal left-handed reliever, once putting together a string of forty-seven scoreless innings. He still holds the school save record (twenty-three).

As good as Helton was, Peyton Manning put on the best show in Knoxville, Saturday after Saturday. Peyton and I became friends, earning me a spot as a spectator on the sidelines at Neyland Stadium—one of the perks of being an athlete—for almost every Tennessee home game. The more I studied him, the more I appreciated what he brought to the field.

Peyton is a good, accurate passer, but his arm doesn't totally wow you. He had nowhere near the arm that Heath Shuler had. Peyton even throws his share of ducks, but it doesn't matter, because everything else is so out of this world that it overrides any little flaw he might have. His decision making, his presence, his gift for leading and making others around him believe—they are all without peer. He is the guy you want in charge, a guy who has been around the game his whole life and it shows. I learned so much from observing him, because it was a constant reminder that the best pitchers are not necessarily the ones who throw the hardest or have the scouts salivating over their arm strength. The best pitchers are the guys who have a plan and know how to execute it.

The first start of my college career pitted us against the University of Miami, one of the country's top programs. I battled hard, but we were down, 3–1, in the middle of the seventh, at which point everything stopped, and not just for "Take Me Out to the Ball

R.A.'S TIPS FOR YOUNG PITCHERS

Practice what you don't do well. *So many of us practice what we are already good at because it makes us feel good about ourselves. Champions have self-awareness. They identify what they need to improve upon and diligently pursue turning a weakness into a strength.*

Game." Lazaro Collazo, the Miami pitching coach, stood behind home plate in his baseball uniform, alongside a clergyman and a woman in a wedding dress. They proceeded to walk beneath a canopy of upraised baseball bats, a sixty-foot-six-inch procession to the pitcher's mound.

I had seen a lot of things happen on ball fields, but that was my first wedding during the seventh-inning stretch. I was happy for the newlyweds but not for me, because—for better or for worse, for richer or for poorer—my start ended with their ceremony. By the time they exchanged vows and rings and got the bats back in the bat rack, almost a half hour had passed.

"You're done, R.A.," the pitching coach told me. "I don't want to send you back out there after such a long delay."

I argued, but *not strenuously enough*. I made a point to remember that. I needed to argue more.

Even as a freshman, I was the staff workhorse, and the owner of a fast-changing body. I had never lifted a weight in my life before I enrolled at Tennessee; suddenly I was lifting all the time, downing creatine, a nutrient that enhances muscle development, before every workout, adding bulk to my quads, hamstrings, and deltoids. I went from 175 pounds to 210 pounds; my fastball accelerated from the 87 to 89 miles per hour range to 93 to 94. I still wasn't a prototypical, strike-out-the-side power pitcher, but I could bring enough heat to make my breaking pitches and changeup more effective.

I wound up winning fifteen straight games after the Collazo wedding, and we made it to the regional finals. I threw seven innings in a victory over Northeastern University on Thursday, then came back on Sunday against Arizona State, a traditional baseball powerhouse. I went ten innings, throwing 140 pitches, before losing on an opposite-field single in the tenth. It was a brutal defeat, but the pain got put in perspective in a hurry. I went over to shake hands with Jim Brock, the legendary Arizona State coach. He was gravely ill with cancer. His body was so full of chemotherapy that his eyes were yellow.

"Congratulations, Coach Brock. Good luck in the College World Series. I will keep you in my prayers," I said. Arizona State beat Miami, but was eliminated by Oklahoma, the ultimate winner.

Coach Brock died four days after the College World Series ended.

I was named an All-American as a freshman, a tremendous honor, but probably made less of an impression on my own campus than I did with baseball scouts. Like at MBA, I made friends but didn't let anybody get too close. As long as you don't let anyone get close, you can't get hurt. I didn't think that consciously; I just lived that way, like a fugitive who doesn't know what he's running from.

R.A.'S TIPS FOR YOUNG PITCHERS

Strengthen your arm. *An exercise routine that includes moderate, sustained weight-lifting will make your arm stronger and help protect against injury. Playing long toss with a partner before every practice or game will keep your arm muscles flexible.*

But no breaking pitches until your teen years! *Before you hit your teen years, your growth plates are still in the process of settling. Fastballs, changeups, and the knuckleball are your friends when you're still a kid pitcher because they put much less stress on the crucial joints in your shoulder and elbow. If you insist on throwing breaking pitches (curveballs, sliders) before age twelve, limit the number to 10 percent of the total pitches thrown.*

The one thing I never ran away from was work. Indeed, I piled it on, determined to be the hardes-working guy on the team. My freshman experience reinforced my feeling that, short of having Sandy Koufax–caliber stuff, the greatest attribute a pitcher can have is a willingness to compete. Without an out pitch, a weapon I could turn to again and again when things got stressful, I had to be aggressive with my fastball and inventive with my other pitches. I had to be a bulldog, which isn't so much a strategy as it is a mentality.

You know how hitters talk about never giving away an at-bat? I don't ever want to give away a single pitch. Even if I'm getting belted around, I want every pitch to have conviction behind it. I want it to be a pitch I'm bringing as a personal challenge to the hitter: Let's see what you can do with this. I've always believed talent is overrated and will is underrated. Or, as Uncle Ricky used to tell me over and over: "The mental is to the physical as four is to one." I was learning that he was right again.

At the end of my sophomore year, we needed to win two games in the regional finals to advance to the College World Series. Dave Serrano, my pitching coach, gave me the ball Thursday and I went seven innings before he pulled me with the victory in hand.

"We're going to need all you've got on Sunday," he reminded me. Our opponent in the regional final was Oklahoma State. A record crowd of 5,086 turned out for the game at our home field. We scored in the third to go up by a run before Oklahoma State tied it up in the bottom of the eighth. I'd thrown about 150 pitches by then. Serrano came to me in the dugout.

"Great job, R.A. Really great job. We're going to let the bullpen take it from here," he said.

I looked right back at him. "You are not taking me out of this game." I made sure to speak in a tone that telegraphed: This is not negotiable.

Serrano walked away. I went out for the ninth. After the ninth he approached me again. "That's it," he said. "You are done."

I am capable of being a complete idiot when it comes to leaving games. I can be as stubborn as a donkey, refusing to listen to reason or heed authority, which was exactly how I behaved that day.

"I am not coming out of this game," I told him. Serrano told me later that I had the wild-eyed look of a guy in the middle of a war who refuses to put his gun down.

I retired Oklahoma State in the tenth, and when I came into the dugout, Serrano collared me and insisted, emphatically, that my day was done. He was losing patience. He told me he had never been a win-at-all-costs guy and he wasn't going to start. "You've pitched your butt off, but I'm not going to risk hurting your arm. You've got a lot of years ahead of you in this game," he said.

He started to walk away, but I stopped him. "I am not going to let you entrust this game to somebody else," I said. "I don't care what you say. I am finishing this game. This game is mine. Nobody else's. I feel fine, feel great. I'm going as long as it takes."

Serrano came right back at me, letting me know I was not in charge. By that point, we were nose to nose, bumping into each other. There wasn't going to be a dugout rumble, but it was a major confrontation in the biggest game of the year.

I walked away, still muttering. "I am finishing this game. That's it. It's mine."

Coach Serrano didn't respond. I figured I'd finally worn him out.

In the top half of the eleventh, we took a 3–1 lead. (Oklahoma State was the home team for that game, and if they had beaten us to force a second game, then we would be the home team.)

I had to get three more outs.

I retired the first guy, but then Rusty McNamara, the Oklahoma State left fielder and number two hitter, worked me for a walk. Not what I wanted to do in that spot—put the tying run at the plate. Next up was Peter Prodanov, the shortstop. He was a right-handed hitter and a good stick, so I reminded myself to be careful, but the guy I really didn't want to face was in the on-deck circle: Tal Light, their designated hitter. Tal could tie up the game with one swing, and then I'd have to fight Coach Serrano to come back out for the twelfth. I needed to end it by getting Prodanov to hit into a groundout, if possible.

I threw a two-seam fastball away and he went with it, making pretty good contact, hitting a high-bounding ball to first. But Todd Helton snared it just over his head and ran to the bag for the second out, then fired to second to try to get McNamara, who beat the throw but overslid the bag. Shortstop Matt Whitley put the tag on him.

The game was over, giving Tennessee its first spot in the College World Series in forty-four years. The whole team rushed to the mound, engulfing me. It was one of the greatest thrills of my career. In the pile, Dave Serrano gave me a hug.

"You are the most stubborn kid I have ever coached,

do you know that?" he asked. "Nobody is even a close second." I could see the conflict on his face, the pride he felt for one of his pitchers coming through in a big moment, and the regret he had that he allowed a kid to bully him out of a decision.

I found out later that I threw 183 pitches.

With Helton departing for pro ball after being selected eighth overall by the Colorado Rockies in the June 1995 draft, head coach Rod Delmonico had to replace our best hitter and a dominant closer. I couldn't help with the hitting, but a month into my junior year, Delmonico tired of us blowing late leads and made me a closer.

The bullpen agreed with me from the start. I loved the challenge and the pressure, the whole hair-on-fire urgency that comes with closing. I loved being able to try to blow the doors off without having to worry about pacing myself over nine—or eleven—innings. In back-to-back outings, I hit 96 miles per hour on the radar gun, my highest reading ever.

Before the year was out, though, I was back in the rotation, because we weren't getting many late-inning leads for me to protect. We just didn't have enough to make another run to the College World Series. I finished my college career the same way I began it, with a loss on the road, this time to Clemson in the NCAA regionals, minus the seventh-inning wedding ceremony. In between those two losses, I won a school-record thirty-eight games and pitched a record 434 innings.

I was sad the year didn't end on a better note, but it wasn't possible to stay down for long. The big-league draft was approaching, and the Olympics. There was a lot going on, a big adventure and a big unknown ahead of me. I thought of Henry Wadsworth Longfellow and words of his I learned in a nineteenth-century literature course along the way:

Go forth to meet the shadowy Future, without fear, and with a manly heart.

Why I Read

Fact: I would never have won the Cy Young if it weren't for reading. People are usually surprised when I make this claim, but I believe it's true. I wear my love of books like a badge. When a reporter wrote about me, "He reads like Jeff Francoeur talks, like José Reyes smiles, like Dan Warthen frets," I took it as a compliment. My corner of the Mets locker room was dubbed "The Library," because John Maine and I chilled out before a game by delving into books.

Most players have each of their bats numbered, so if they break one, or want a different one, they can tell the batboy, "Get me No. 2." My bats are named for mythical swords from literature. I like to use Orcrist the Goblin Cleaver from The Hobbit if I'm going to try to bunt for a single. If the plan is to swing away and loop the ball over the infielders' heads, I might select Hrunting, a sword mentioned in the epic poem Beowulf. (I wrote each bat's name on the knob, so the bat boys can figure out which is which.)

R.A. doesn't stand for "reads a lot," but it could. I gravitate toward stories about people who have overcome great obstacles to realize their dreams or to reach a desired goal. Those stories *have helped me grow my own sense of what's possible in life.*

Reading is like fertilizer for your imagination, and it took a lot of imagination to picture myself as a knuckleballer when I had spent two decades of my baseball life trying to throw the ball as hard and as fast as I could. I had to believe that I could achieve great things by taking a very different path. Reading other people's stories of beating the odds inspired me. It helped me believe I could become someone different.

Reading improved my imagination. A big imagination allowed me to dream big. Dreaming big brought me to . . . the Cy Young Award.

Nice formula, don't you think?

Chapter 7

OLYMPIC DREAMS

I had no doubt that the summer of 1996 was going to be the best time of my life. After finishing my junior year at Tennessee, I joined my other teammates on Team USA, preparing for the upcoming Olympic Games in Atlanta. It was my third summer playing for the national team. Team USA was housed in a Navy barracks in Millington, Tennessee. A short walk down the hallway took me past the rooms of the best collegiate players in the country: Kris Benson of Clemson, Mark Kotsay of Cal State–Fullerton, Braden Looper of Wichita State, Travis Lee of San Diego State, and Jeff Weaver of Fresno State.

I also had my eye on the Major League Baseball free-agent draft, which takes place every year in June. That year draft day was scheduled for the first Tuesday in June. I dreamed of playing in the big leagues since I was a seven-year-old kid who wanted to be the next Nolan Ryan. Now that dream was right around the corner. I tried to act like it was no big deal, but the truth was that my whole future revolved around the outcome of the draft. It was huge. It was everything.

People in the know predicted I would be the first-round draft choice of a big-league organization. That meant, by the end of the summer, hopefully after an Olympic gold medal, I would have a big check to deposit in the bank. I could buy Anne an engagement ring and ask her to marry me.

I actually had my first experience in the draft when I graduated from high school in 1993. The Detroit Tigers selected me in the tenth round, but Uncle Ricky advised that unless their offer was ridiculously generous, I should go to college (which was what I wanted to do anyway). I wasn't ready for pro ball at nineteen. Now three years later, I was draft eligible again. Scouts had been following me the previous couple of years, trying to gauge how I stacked up against the other pitchers available. Start after start, I auditioned for guys I'd never met, people who would have a massive impact on my future. They had their notebooks and radar guns and organizational hats. Their job was to determine if an athlete was worthy of using the team's first-round pick. It's the meat-market part of the business, and if they like another cut of meat better than you, you stay in the display case a while longer. It all comes down to what they write up in their reports and how they grade you.

Literally.

Part of the package is a psychological-profile exam, something teams use to assess your makeup and character. You get multiple-choice questions like this:

You take a two-hit shutout into the bottom of the ninth, only to lose when your second baseman boots two consecutive grounders. You deal with the situation by:

A. Taking a bat to the watercooler in the dugout.

B. Telling a reporter—on the record—that the manager screwed up by not putting in the backup second baseman, who has a better glove.

C. Brooding at your locker with a towel over your head, just to make sure everybody knows how heartbreaking the game was for you.

D. Making a point to go over to the second baseman and say, "Hey, forget the ninth inning. You can play second base behind me anytime."

I always made sure to give answers that I thought would score me character points, not necessarily the truthful answers. In other words, I lied, when necessary. But on this question, I didn't have to fib: No way would I bury a guy because he made an error. In life, and on the exam, I go for answer D.

I know this probably sounds straight out of Cornball Central, but there's nothing corny about loyalty to me. The day I don't stand by my teammates is the day I don't want to play anymore. Besides, I like it when guys stand by me after I screw up.

I woke up anxious in my barracks on draft day. How could I not be anxious? My life was about to change, perhaps in some momentous way. From what I'd heard, the Oakland A's had the most interest. They had scouted me frequently and the team had the tenth pick in the first round. I imagined myself in green and gold, pitching for an organization that had been home to big-time pitchers like Catfish Hunter, Vida Blue, and Dave Stewart. I heard the Bay Area was nice. I had made up my mind that Oakland would be a great fit.

The A's used their pick to take a high school third baseman named Eric Chavez.

Oh, well. The Bay Area is too cold, anyway.

I wound up going to the Texas Rangers. (Let's hear it for heat.) The Rangers took me with the eighteenth pick, right after the Cubs took a high school pitcher from Louisiana named Todd Noel. I found myself wondering about Todd, what his story was, and how he got to be a first-round pick in the major leagues. I wondered how many of the top guys in the draft would wind up being stars and which ones would never be heard from again.

I wondered how I measured up against them. Would I ever be heard from again?

Every slot you drop in the first round costs you money—hundreds of thousands of dollars of money—so it wasn't good that I slipped to eighteen. The word I got was that the scouts were concerned that I was overused at Tennessee and that my velocity had dropped from the mid-nineties to the low nineties over the previous month or two. When a young pitcher loses velocity, he might as well have a contagious disease; it usually makes teams run in the other direction. In that sense, I was fortunate to still be in the first round.

So how could I be unhappy? The Rangers had barely scouted me because they didn't think I'd still be around when they got to pick. Now I'd be in the same organization as Nolan Ryan, not to mention Jonathan Johnson, one of my best friends, whom the Rangers had taken in the first round a year earlier.

With the draft complete, I dove back into my life on Team USA, preparing for the Atlanta Olympics.

The Olympics experience is like no other, and not just the competition aspect of it. When we arrived in Atlanta, one perk was a visit to a warehouse-size facility, where the shelves were loaded down with swag. Every athlete was given a shopping cart and invited to help himself to whatever he needed—shoes, sweatshirts, warm-up suits, shorts, T-shirts, an official Opening Ceremony outfit, luggage, even a 10K gold Olympic ring. All free.

Also, Olympic athletes never went hungry. In the Olympic Village (on the campus of Georgia Tech), food was served all day, every day, and the cuisine was completely international. Craving a quesadilla at two a.m.? No problem. In the mood for mu shu pork mid-afternoon? That could easily be satisfied.

Did I mention it was also free?

You could even get your hair cut at the Olympic Village barber. Cost: Free.

In two weeks chock-full of memories, perhaps the most remarkable one was the Opening Ceremony. Because we were the host country, we entered Centennial Olympic Stadium last, and the baseball players were lined up alongside the "Dream Team III," the USA basketball squad that was comprised of some of the top players ever to play roundball—Shaquille O'Neal, Charles Barkley, David Robinson, Karl Malone, Scottie Pippen, John Stockton, and Hakeem Olajuwon. When we jogged into the stadium, the roar of approval was just deafening. It was more incredible than I ever imagined it would be.

If I hadn't been all-in before that, now I was not only a competitor at the 1996 Olympics, but an insatiable fan. I collected pins, traded practice jerseys with athletes from other countries, and got to as many events as my own schedule would allow. Warren Morris, our second baseman, and I were in the Georgia Dome when gymnast Kerri Strug landed her famous vault (on one leg—she had damaged tendons in the other leg on her first vault) to secure the first-ever team gold medal for the "Magnificent Seven" of USA women's gymnastics. At Olympic Stadium, I saw Michael Johnson, considered one of the greatest sprinters in the history of track and field, leave his competitors in the dust as he set world records in the 200- and 400-meter dash.

Of course, the members of the baseball team were no slouches. We had a lineup loaded with big bats and a starting rotation that consisted of five of the top collegiate pitchers in the country: Kris Benson, Billy Koch, Braden Looper, Seth Greisinger, and me. People were calling it one of the best pitching staffs Team USA had ever had. I was the least acclaimed of the five, but that's okay. On July 22, 1996, *Baseball America* put all of us on the cover before the Games began. It was a huge honor to be showcased on the cover of the bible of amateur baseball. The headline read "Armed for Battle." I made sure Anne and my mom saved copies for my scrapbook.

This is a press clip I am never going to forget, I told myself.

Team USA's coach was Skip Bertman of LSU, one of the most inspirational coaches I've ever been around. Skip was always showing us film clips or giving speeches, finding novel ways to fire us up. He called us together one day in the locker room during the pre-Olympic tour.

Skip previously had given each of us a crystal baseball paperweight as a keepsake. He stood before us holding his own paperweight. He talked about the Olympics and the opportunity before us, and how important it was to put the team above all else. Suddenly the quiet of the room shattered when Skip purposely let his ball drop onto the floor, the crystal exploding on impact, startling everybody.

"A team is a very special thing," Skip said. "It's something to cherish, to preserve, but it's also fragile, like the crystal ball I just dropped, because once it's broken or fractured—once guys don't stay together and start playing the blame game and splitting up—you can try to glue or patch it and reassemble it, but it's never the same. Never. So be a team. Stay together. If you do that, you can do great things."

I loved his message. We believed we were capable of the greatest thing of all in the Olympic baseball orbit: beating Cuba for the gold medal. We played Cuba four times the year before, in 1995, and beat them four times. Teams comprised of US college kids were not supposed to do that against the Cubans, longtime kings of amateur baseball.

Our bats were on fire as round-robin play began. We hit five home runs in the first inning of a 15–5 blowout of Japan, one of the medal favorites. I started against Italy and we won, 15–3. Not exactly the 1927 Yankees as an opponent, but I felt good about how I performed after a rocky first inning. For the whole tournament, we averaged four homers per game and lost only once, 10–8, to Cuba, in a tight preliminary-round game, before heading into the semifinals against Japan.

We had confidence. We believed we could handle Cuba when we faced them next, and we'd beaten Japan the last nine times we'd played them, and I mean thrashed them, most of the time.

Were we overconfident? The Japanese scored three

R.A.'S TIPS FOR YOUNG PITCHERS

Be a good teammate. *This goes back to the Golden Rule we all learned in kindergarten: Treat others the way you yourself would like to be treated. Encourage and support your teammates, and hopefully they will do the same for you, even when you have a bad day on the mound.*

in the second inning against Benson, our starter and the number one pick in the entire big-league draft that summer. They scored three more in the fifth, ultimately hitting five home runs against our pitching. Meanwhile, we somehow turned a pitcher named Masanori Sugiura into the Japanese Greg Maddux. Sugiura's regular team was the Nippon Life Insurance Company, and his policy on that day was to put every pitch just where he wanted it.

We fell behind 6–0, then 8–2 and 10–2. I was in the bullpen for the game, thinking I was going to throw up. I mean it. I was physically nauseous—that's how revolted I was by what was going on, as if I had food poisoning.

The final score was 11–2. Japan advanced to the gold-medal game against the Cubans. Team USA would play for the bronze against Nicaragua.

It hurt more than any defeat I'd ever been involved in.

The next day Skip told us that even though that wasn't the game we wanted to play, we owed it to our Maker, families, and country to honor the game and play hard. We scored four in the top of the first and won 10–3. Cuba beat Japan, 13–9, for the gold. When the bronze medal was placed around my neck, it was the most bittersweet moment of my sporting career. I finished my year with

Team USA undefeated, 7-0, with a 3.35 earned run average. I was proud to win an Olympic medal for my country. But I was incredibly disappointed that the medal wasn't gold, and that the national anthem they played during the medal ceremony wasn't "The Star-Spangled Banner."

I packed up my stuff and my swirling emotions and headed back to Nashville, waiting for my agent to hammer out a deal with the Rangers so I could start my new life as a professional pitcher.

Chapter 8

ARM TROUBLE

I had a million-dollar arm. That's what Lloyd's of London thought, anyway. Lloyd's is a company that specializes in insuring rare, odd, and priceless entities. At the suggestion of my coaches at Tennessee, I insured my arm with Lloyd's during my sophomore year, just in case I got hurt and never had a professional career. The insurance cost $30,000, but Lloyd's let me defer the payments until I signed with a big-league club.

I didn't like owing this kind of money to anybody, so the first debt I planned to pay when I got my signing bonus was to Lloyd's. After a lot of back-and-forth, the Rangers offered $810,000. My agent at the time, Mark Rodgers, thought this was fair, so I accepted it.

I said a prayer of thanks to God and began planning my first expenditures—the money I owed Lloyd's, an engagement ring for Anne, and something special for my mother and sister, Jane.

The thought of having that kind of money boggled

my mind. I started life in a cockroach-infested apartment with forks from the Western Sizzlin. Now I was on the verge of being 81 percent of the way to the millionaire club (less my agent's commission, of course). I tried to imagine signing the contract with my name and that number on it, but I couldn't. The bigger thrill, honestly, was what was attached to the money: a big-league career.

Mark and I flew to Dallas so I could take the mandatory physical and sign the contract. The Rangers wanted me to meet Nolan Ryan and throw out the first pitch at the game that night. The whole flight down, I was mesmerized by the thought of standing on the mound in The Ballpark, with Ryan in the wings and tens of thousands of people cheering.

There was no other way to think about it: It was going to be one of the greatest moments of my life.

When we got to Texas, I went straight to see the team orthopedist, Dr. John Conway. The doctor knew about me already, from the Olympics and from Danny Wheat, the Rangers' trainer. In the clubhouse one day, Wheat saw the *Baseball America* cover, where I was posed, sideways, with the other Team USA starters.

Wheat pointed the photo out to Conway. "His arm kind of looks like it's hanging at a weird angle, doesn't it?" he asked. "This kid is our number one draft choice and he already looks like he's got elbow problems."

The other pitchers' right arms were hanging straighter than mine, which had a slight bend at the elbow.

Conway agreed it looked a bit odd, and filed that information away.

Now I was in his office, contorting my arm in various directions. I thought: This guy's being thorough, but I also figured that's standard operating procedure where there's a lot of money involved.

Everything checked out fine, as far as I knew. The last test Conway administered was the valgus stress test. He placed my arm in a snug-fitting apparatus, then had me twist my wrist back and forth as an X-ray machine filmed what was going on inside. After the test, he put the X-ray on a light box, to illuminate it. It looked like a normal elbow to me.

"You have a couple of millimeters of extra laxity in there," Conway said.

"What does that mean?" I wondered.

"It means there is a little extra play in there that isn't normal," he said.

"That doesn't matter, does it?" My anxiety level was rising, but I was determined to keep my cool and convince him there was nothing wrong. "My arm doesn't hurt. I've never missed a start. I throw the ball in the nineties. I don't see how that could matter if I have no symptoms."

"I don't know," Conway said. "It's hard to say."

We shook hands and Mark and I left, headed next to see Doug Melvin, the Rangers' general manager. "I don't like what he said about the laxity," Mark confided. "I hope it's not a problem."

"I'm as healthy as can be," I assured him. That wasn't just me blowing smoke, either. I know my body better than anybody, and my arm felt great.

At The Ballpark, we took the elevator to the team's executive offices, which overlook the field in left center. Doug poked his head out and asked to speak to Mark. I walked onto the balcony for a bird's-eye view of my future place of employment. It looked spectacular: the richest, most verdant grass I'd ever seen.

I wanted to be on that mound, facing a big-league hitter. Now.

Below me, in the bullpen, Roger Pavlik, a Rangers pitcher, was having a side session. His cleats were bright red, as cool as any shoes I'd ever seen on a ballplayer.

It would be awesome to wear red cleats, I thought. I looked up at the empty seats and took in the size of the place, trying to imagine what it would be like to pitch there one day soon. I felt a gratitude so immense, I prayed out loud: "Thank you, Lord, for all your blessings and for helping me get this far."

My prayer was still in the air when I saw Mark walking toward me, his face whiter than home plate.

"You need to come in to Doug's office," he said.

I had no idea what was happening, but I knew immediately it wasn't good. Doug is a Canadian with a thick mustache and a solid build, like a guy who might be a Mountie if he wasn't running a baseball team. He had a stern, distant look on his face.

"We are going to retract our offer," he said. "We think there's something wrong with your elbow and we want to have further testing done."

His face showed no emotion whatsoever. This was business. All business.

I had trouble taking in his words: "We are going to retract our offer."

Could I have heard him wrong?

As the words sank in, my anger rose. Not anger. Rage. Complete rage. It started in my toes and blasted upward through my body, like a volcano erupting into my gut, blowing straight through the top of my head.

I had an urge, as strong as anything I had ever felt,

to reach across the desk and strangle that man who quietly and dispassionately had just ripped apart everything I'd worked for, my whole life's dream, and crushed it as if it were a bug on the pavement. I wanted to cuss and tell this man exactly who he was stomping on. Part of me wanted to tell him about all the ways my life was screwed up and how baseball was the one thing, the only thing, I could do right. The thing that made me somebody.

I wanted to make sure he knew how it felt to be me after he matter-of-factly dropped this atomic bomb on my baseball career. On my life.

But first I wanted to get on his side of the desk and let him know how it felt to be pummeled worse than he'd ever been pummeled in his life.

But I did not leave my chair. It was as if there was a strong hand on my shoulder holding me back. In an instant I had self-control that wasn't there a moment earlier.

I heard a voice: *Relax, R.A. It's going to be okay.*

I was just talking to God on the balcony and now He was talking back, bestowing on me a composure that could not have come from anywhere else.

I was crushed by Doug Melvin's words, but I would not do anything stupid.

I got up slowly. I didn't say a word. I walked out with Mark and passed the balcony without stopping to look at the field or Roger Pavlik or his red shoes. I was in a complete daze, almost as though I didn't know who or where I was or what just happened, as if my whole life's hard drive had been wiped out.

Mark drove me to the airport. He tried to boost my spirits, but that wasn't going to happen and we both knew it. We passed through security, walking amid all these people going places and living their lives. None of whom knew or cared what had just happened to me, a little laxity leaving me as shattered as Skip Bertman's crystal baseball. I got on my plane, the rage dissipating, replaced by a terrible loneliness. I left Nashville that morning, full of excitement. I returned that afternoon, full of despair.

"We are going to retract our offer." Doug Melvin's words replayed on a continuous loop in my head.

I looked out the window at thirty thousand feet, searching for comfort, any comfort at all, and remembered God had words for me too.

It's going to be okay.

Chapter 9

THE MISSING LI ... GAMENT

In my despair, I almost forgot about the other words Doug Melvin said, about getting additional testing done on my elbow. The Rangers sent me to see Dr. James Andrews in Birmingham, Alabama.

Andrews has long been the go-to guy for major-league pitchers with arm problems. Photos of his most famous patients—from Roger Clemens to John Smoltz—decorate his office walls. When he examined my elbow, he didn't see any real problems. "The attrition in it is a little worse than most guys your age, but that's understandable because you've thrown a lot more than most guys," he said. "Let's go ahead and take an MRI while you're here and make sure we're all good and then we'll be done with you."

That gave me hope. It sounded like Andrews might be able to report to the Rangers that everything checked out. My offer would be back on the table.

A technician injected my arm with a dye and I got

inside the MRI tube, where I had to lie perfectly still for forty-five minutes while listening to the loud jackhammering sound the machine made.

By the time I finished and went back to Andrews's office, a cluster of doctors in white jackets were having a lively discussion in front of a screen, looking at the MRI image of my elbow. I walked over to listen, but Dr. Andrews got to me first.

"I can't find the existence of an ulnar collateral ligament in your elbow," he said.

The UCL—a thick, triangular band of tissue—is the main stabilizing ligament in the elbow. Without it, the elbow should be about as stable as a car without a steering wheel.

"I've looked at thousands of these," he explained. "I've seen torn UCLs and frayed UCLs. I've done a million Tommy John surgeries to repair UCLs. I've never in my life seen an elbow with no UCL at all."

So much for hope. So much for all my prayers. To Dr. Andrews, I was a clinical marvel, a freak of nature. Check it out! See the pitcher with no UCL! I could join the circus, but I couldn't get my offer back from the Texas Rangers.

Andrews theorized that I could've been born without the UCL in my right elbow, though it's more likely that

I injured it when I was young and it withered up and died at some point. He couldn't believe that I wasn't in extreme discomfort. Nor could he believe that I could throw the ball pretty much where I wanted. "It should hurt to turn a doorknob, to shake hands, to do the most routine of tasks," he said.

Dr. Andrews's disbelief only made me feel worse. He was so confounded, in fact, that he ordered a second MRI.

By this point, I was barely holding it together. When the jackhammering started again, I thought I might have a full-blown anxiety attack. I distracted myself by coming up with arguments to make to Doug Melvin.

Because I don't have a UCL, that means it can never get torn or hurt. Think of the reassurance that comes with that. Maybe I should be worth even more money!

I was not so naïve to think that argument would fly.

MRI number two showed nothing different. It confirmed I was a pitcher without the one indispensable stabilizing ligament that you need to throw a baseball.

After I left, Andrews called the Rangers and delivered the shocking news. Of course, he was obligated to recommend that the team not sign me. After all, I was not what I seemed to be. I was damaged goods.

The dream crushing was now complete. What I felt

above everything else was the epic unfairness of it. Drafted in the first round, offered all this money, only to have it yanked away because of a one-in-a-billion medical condition.

I prayed to God for understanding, but the truth was, I had very little understanding. I was angry at God, angry at the Rangers, angry at the world. The whole thing tapped into old wounds about being damaged in a deep way even if the world couldn't see it.

I am the Pitcher Without an Ulnar Collateral Ligament.

Newspaper sports sections had a field day reporting on this oddity. Tabloid TV shows wanted to do a segment on me. The bizarre tale swept through baseball. Did you hear about that kid the Rangers took in the first round? Can you believe there's a pitcher who doesn't have a UCL?

I returned to Nashville and holed up at the Bartholomews' house. Where would I go from there? No team was going to touch me after Dr. Andrews's evaluation. My best option was to go back to Tennessee for my senior year, to finish my degree. Maybe if I had another strong season, a club would take a chance on me, UCL or no UCL.

I was still weighing my choices when the phone

rang at the Bartholomews' one afternoon. My future mother-in-law, Vicki, answered it. From the next room, I heard her voice rising. She sounded as though she was going to start cussing. I had never heard a cuss word escape from her mouth.

"How could you do this to this young man?" she barked at whoever it was she was talking to. "Do you know how cruel this is, to take his dream and rip it up in his face? Do you have any heart at all?"

I walked over, hoping to calm her down. I appreciated her speaking up for me, but I wondered who was getting the earful. She handed me the phone. "It's someone from the Rangers," she said. "I think his name is Nolan."

No, it couldn't be. Don't tell me that Vicki just dressed down a Hall of Famer and my hero. Please don't tell me that. I took the phone.

"Hey, R.A. It's Nolan Ryan," he said. "I can see y'all have some people there who are upset about things, and I don't blame them. I was just calling to tell you I'm sorry the way things happened. I sure hope you stay with it and things work out for the best for you."

Nolan went on to tell me that he pitched the last five or six years with a messed-up ulnar collateral ligament. He talked about all the people who doubted him when he was a young pitcher who couldn't throw strikes. We talked for five minutes and I told him that I appreciated his call, apologizing that he got an earful when he was just trying to do something nice. "Don't worry about it," he said.

A week passed. I re-enrolled at Tennessee and chose my classes. My senior year was set to begin the next day with a nine a.m. class in nineteenth-century American literature. Once I stepped foot in that classroom, I would be committed to school and not able to sign with a pro team until the following June. I was getting my books together when my agent called, telling me he had just spoken with Doug Melvin, who had been "rethinking my situation."

Melvin had called his own father to ask for advice. His father told him: You can't just cut this kid loose and not give him anything. You owe him something—even if it's nowhere near the eight hundred thousand you were going to give him.

Melvin decided his dad was right, so the Rangers would sign me, if I would take $75,000. The offer included an invitation to big-league training camp. It was a take-it-or-leave-it proposition.

Mark and I didn't talk long. The missing UCL had officially cost me $735,000. The Rangers' new offer was more like fifteenth-round money than first-round money, but in the Rangers' mind, that's about where I belonged.

I accepted it, and withdrew from Tennessee. I held a press conference at Montgomery Bell Academy so I could go through the whole mess once and not have to answer questions for weeks on end. I rolled out every platitude I could think of about adversity and about how champions are people who rise above it. I said I wasn't sad or discouraged about my big offer being retracted, a naked lie.

I used the bonus money to buy an engagement ring for Anne, pay off my Lloyd's of London premium, and take care of some of my father's debts. In early October, I borrowed a truck to drive fourteen hours from Nashville to Port Charlotte, Florida, where the Rangers had their instructional league team.

I had $7,000 left.

Chapter 10

MINOR ACHIEVEMENT

Like any prospect, I hoped to spend as little time as possible in the minor leagues. Succeed, advance, and say good-bye to bus rides forever. That was my game plan, and after the emotional roller coaster that was 1996, I was determined to make it happen. I planned to outwork every human being on the planet. I would do whatever it took to make it.

That was the face I put on for the world, anyway.

Secretly, I felt more insecure than ever. For as long as I'd been in sports—as a pitcher in baseball or a forward in basketball or a quarterback in football—I'd never had anybody tell me I couldn't do something. I'd lost games and missed shots and thrown interceptions, of course, but mostly I'd delivered, and been applauded for it.

Now, for the first time, somebody—the Texas Rangers—had doubted me, opening my own personal floodgate of worry. What if I couldn't do it? What would my life be like without baseball?

I reread press clippings from my days at Tennessee, about big games I won and about being named an All-American. I needed to convince myself that I was the same guy, capable of the same success. In the mirror, I still saw R. A. Dickey. Six feet two inches, 215 pounds. Throws right, bats right.

You can do this, I told myself. You can show the whole world that UCLs are way overrated.

It was a tough sell.

My first full year as a professional ballplayer didn't do much to restore my confidence. It ended after eight appearances, six starts, and thirty-five innings in the Florida State League, cut short by bone chips in my right elbow. They're painful but not particularly serious. I got an arthroscopic cleanup—totally unrelated to the absence of a UCL—and was anxious for spring training to begin.

But first, I married Anne Bartholomew on December 13, 1997, before an intimate gathering of five hundred people, including two former governors and a 1996 Republican presidential candidate—the type of men whom my new father-in-law, a prominent Nashville lawyer, moves with.

Our entertaining became a lot less extravagant from that point on.

If you want to get by on a minor-league salary, you need to watch every penny. When we moved to Port Charlotte, Florida, where the Rangers hold spring training, we took one car, and started married life sharing an apartment with another couple so we could split the $650 rent. Anne got one job at a clothing store and another teaching aerobics.

To boost our income, I started a business venture with my friend Jonathan Johnson, another Rangers pitcher and the best man at our wedding. It was our night job (so no one would see us) retrieving wayward golf balls from ponds and lakes at local golf courses.

We invested in rope and rakes with little baskets at the end that allowed us to scoop up a dozen or more balls at a time. More than occasionally, however, the rake got stuck on something and either Jonathan or I would have to dive in to free it from the mucky bottom. We actively ignored the fact that, by daylight, you could see some pretty significant hazards to this plan, sunning themselves on the banks of every pond and lake we frequented. But when it was my turn underwater I always had an uneasy premonition about possible embarrassing headlines like:

RANGERS' PROSPECT EATEN BY ALLIGATORS WHILE FISHING FOR GOLF BALLS IN LAGOON

This would be right up there with the most ridiculous baseball injuries of all time, alongside Cardinals outfielder Vince Coleman getting his leg mashed by a mechanical tarp and Braves reliever Cecil Upshaw suffering a career-ending injury supposedly while practicing imaginary dunks on an awning.

Luckily, gators must be American League fans. We repeatedly made the rounds of three golf courses, collecting thousands of golf balls. Back at the apartment, we scrubbed the balls with bleach to get them as white as possible. We packaged them by the dozen in athletic socks lifted from the clubhouse, separated by brand—Titleists, Maxflis, Nikes—a sock for every budget. Our best customer was probably pitcher Kenny Rogers, a Titleist man, who paid us ten dollars for a dozen. Will Clark was a regular customer too.

By the time spring training ended, we'd made

$3,000. Jonathan, who got a $1.1 million signing bonus, insisted I keep all of it, even though he worked as hard or harder than me, diving to the bottom of all those lagoons.

"I don't think that's fair," I told him. "You were in the water with those gators more than I was."

"Nobody's keeping score," he said.

R.A.'S TIPS FOR YOUNG PITCHERS

Nothing beats a good game of catch. *By catch, I mean an intentional exercise to pick out a target on your catching partner (his cap, a letter on his shirt, etc.) and aim for it. Do things with a purpose. Yes, you are trying to loosen up your arm, but also get in the habit of training your eye to throw a ball that hits a target.*

Late that spring, a player-development executive pulled me aside to tell me the Rangers had an experiment in mind.

"We want to give you a look as a closer," he said.

This was a couple of days before the regular season started, but I said nothing, just reported to the bullpen, same as I had done at Tennessee. If that's where the Rangers thought I could help, that's where I'd pitch.

In fact, I saved thirty-eight games and made the All-Star team, ensuring a move up to Double-A ball in Tulsa in 1999.

The major leagues were now just two steps away.

Chapter 11

THE SHOW

I spent the 1999 season splitting my time between Double-A Tulsa and Triple-A Oklahoma City. I started the 2000 season on the Oklahoma RedHawks' roster.

Four years after the draft, the major leagues were finally just one step away.

I began the year in the bullpen and got knocked around a little, before I was moved into the rotation at the end of April, and proceeded to lose my first four starts. I finally started getting guys out with some consistency in late May and June.

Anne and I had a one-bedroom apartment next to a Dumpster. It had a rented couch and a coffee table made from a cardboard box with a bedsheet thrown over it. Lifestyles of the broke and anonymous.

A year later, we were still there. This time, I began the season by winning my first two starts.

My third game was likely going to be a tougher

outing. We were playing the Sky Sox in Colorado Springs, in a ballpark that makes Coors Field seem like a pitcher's paradise. Balls don't just fly out in the thin air of Colorado Springs. They get launched. From a pitcher's perspective, it's the worst place on the planet to start a baseball game. I was at my locker thinking about how to avoid destroying my ERA when a familiar voice called out, "Dewclaw Dickey."

The speaker was Lee Tunnell, the RedHawks' pitching coach and the guy who gave me the nickname. Lee had been calling me Dewclaw for the previous year because of a popular fan promotion in the Pacific Coast League, called Dog Day or Bark in the Park, which allowed fans to bring their dogs to the game. During the 2000 season, there were a bunch of Dog Days at various parks around the PCL, and I seemed to be the starting pitcher for every single one.

If dogs were in the house, Dickey was on the mound.

Lee could've called me Dog Day Dickey, or 3-D, but for some reason he latched on to Dewclaw, the term used to describe a dog's extra (and rather useless) claw. I'd show up to pitch at that week's Bark in the Park event, and Lee would say, "Go get 'em today, Dewclaw." That's how it began.

I wondered if he had advice for me about that day's game.

Instead, he had news to deliver. "They're calling you up," he said.

"No they're not," I told him.

"Yeah they are. They want you there ASAP, so you better get your collar and your chew toys and get your tail to Texas." He grabbed my hand to shake it. "You deserve it, Dewclaw. Now, don't come back."

I had no idea what to say. I'd dreamed of this moment for so long. I was twenty-six years old at that point. In dog years, that's ancient; in baseball, getting close.

The news spread quickly through the shoe box of a clubhouse. Right away I sensed a division as big as Pike's Peak in my teammates' reactions. Most guys were genuinely happy for me. A few could barely conceal their bitterness that they weren't the ones going to the majors. I didn't blame them. I'd been in that position, watching other guys get the call. It's no fun being left behind. It's the dream we all shared, but there are only so many spots in the big leagues, so it's a zero-sum game we play: If you get called up, it means that I didn't. If I get called up, it means you didn't.

But I was not letting somebody's dour expression rob me of one of the best days of my life.

I called Anne, who was ecstatic and promised to figure out a way to meet me in Texas, before I hustled to the airport. At the ticket counter, the agent said, "You will be traveling first-class, Mr. Dickey."

I'd never flown first-class before. But it beat riding the bus, that's for sure.

At The Ballpark, a guard directed me to the Rangers' clubhouse. At the door I stopped to remind myself not to act like some doofus from Dixie on his first trip to the big city.

Be cool, I told myself. It's just a room; a place where guys pull on their jerseys and jockstraps, not some mythical den populated by supermen. My plan was to act as though I'd been in big-league clubhouses a thousand times before, even though I'd never spent one second in a big-league clubhouse.

Yes, sir. I would take coolness to new heights.

I walked in. It took about two seconds for the goose bumps to start popping and my jaw to drop. I was deep in Doofus City.

How bad an actor am I? Very bad.

The sheer size and splendor of the clubhouse—at

least, compared to the frayed carpets and cubbyhole lockers I'd gotten used to—was mind-blowing. The trainer's room looked like a high-end health club. The lounge was the size of a small house. I passed lockers that belonged to the Rodriguezes—Alex and Pudge—Ken Caminiti, Rafael Palmeiro, and Michael Young.

I reached my locker. The nameplate above it read DICKEY, as if I'd been around as long as any of them. Hung on a hook was a white number 51 jersey with my name on the back. Not iron-on. Stitched. It looked too perfect to get sweaty in.

The nameplate in the next locker let me know that space belonged to a veteran right-handed pitcher. He hadn't arrived yet.

I put my stuff in the locker and got changed. I put my shoes on the floor where my space adjoined my fellow right-hander. I was pulling on my socks when he arrived. He saw my shoes, and kicked them to the center of the room. I guess my shoes were trespassing on his territory by a few inches. I looked at him, stunned. His face was angry and hard.

He didn't say, "Hello, welcome to the big leagues," or remark on my shoes encroaching on his space. He said absolutely nothing. I retrieved my shoes and didn't say anything either. I didn't know if anybody else saw his kick, but if they did, they didn't say anything.

Okay, I was a rookie, and I'd been around the game long enough to know about baseball's caste system, where the time-honored custom was for rookies to be as invisible as cellophane. But I don't understand how this benefits anybody. Why do you need to have a certain amount of big-league time to be treated like a human being? Why not make a young guy comfortable? Apart from being the right thing to do, isn't it more likely he'll play better if he has a sense of belonging?

Some baseball customs are downright dumb.

Respect is earned over time; I understand that. It doesn't mean that the people like this veteran had the right to degrade somebody just because he was getting his first shot.

My first big-league opponent was to be the Oakland A's, who were in town for a four-game series. After I was dressed, I walked up the dugout steps out onto the field. I had difficulty believing I'd really made it back to this ballpark. Heading to the bullpen, I realized I was nearing the exact spot where I saw red-shoed Roger

Pavlik throwing a bullpen session five years earlier, just before Doug Melvin retracted my offer.

I felt exhilarated. I felt profoundly grateful. Nobody thought I'd ever be heard of again. I was, after all, damaged goods. The Pitcher Without a UCL.

And now here I was. A major leaguer. For at least a day.

I wanted to believe it might last longer than that, but optimism doesn't come naturally to me.

Anne, my mom, and a dozen other family and friends made the seven-hundred-mile drive from Nashville for the series, but I didn't get in the first three games. By the fourth and final game, on Sunday, the novelty of being in the bullpen had worn off. I was dying to get on the mound, but it wasn't as if I could ask the manager to put me in because my wife and family were in town.

Then we scored four in the third and four in the seventh and were up 11–2. Pudge and Palmeiro homered; A-Rod went three for four. In the top of the eighth, the bullpen phone rang. Bobby Cuellar, the bullpen coach, answered it. The conversation lasted about five seconds.

Cuellar looked at me. "You got the ninth, kid," he said.

I got off the bench and stretched. I started throwing

easily and gradually increased velocity. I felt good. I felt strong. The bottom of the eighth ended. It was time.

When I first met Anne in seventh grade, I told her three things were going to happen:

She and I would get married.

U2 would play at our wedding.

One day, I would be a big-league ballplayer.

I was about to increase my average to .667.

I ran in from the pen, trying not to look at the crowd or the size of the stadium around me, but I couldn't stop myself from stealing a quick glance at the family section, where Anne and my parents were sitting. On my first warm-up pitch to Pudge, my left leg, my front leg, shook like a bowl of jelly. I threw several more pitches and it continued to quiver. Worry threatened to overtake me. What if it didn't stop? What if I had to pitch from the stretch? I'd balk on every pitch. I wondered if any pitcher in history ever had to bail out of a game because of leg tremors.

The first batter up was Mark Bellhorn, the A's third baseman. I looked in for Pudge's sign. Fastball.

The quivering continued.

I wound up and fired the ball over the inner half of

the plate. Bellhorn swung, lifting an easy fly ball to left. One out.

Whoa. That relaxed me. The quivering subsided.

Sal Fasano, the A's catcher, stepped in next. I threw two more fastballs. He popped up the second one behind home plate. Two out.

The next hitter was Mario Valdez, who replaced Jason Giambi at first base in the blowout. I missed with two fastballs and then threw another on 2-0. Valdez swung and popped it up behind third. Alex Rodriguez ran into foul territory, making the catch not too far from the seats.

The ball game was over.

As I watched the third out of my first inning in the big leagues, a perfect inning, settle into A-Rod's glove, I felt a pure, sweet surge of elation. It was just one inning, a mop-up inning at that, but I'd just set down three big-league hitters. A good way to get started.

I kept my eyes fixed on A-Rod because I couldn't wait to get the ball from him and hold it and smell it and then, of course, give it to Anne.

It was the only first ball I would ever have.

I watched Alex Rodriguez take the ball out of his glove. I watched him put it in his right hand. Then I watched him flip the ball—my ball—into the stands. It all unfolded in agonizingly slow motion, the giving away of my keepsake, from glove to palm to a fan I would never see again. A-Rod trotted off the field.

Did I really see that happen? Did A-Rod throw the ball from my first big-league game into the stands?

I was in disbelief. I watched the fan head up the aisle, and as I stood in the infield, accepting congratulations, all I could think of was my lost souvenir. I felt great about the win, but what about my ball?

We finished shaking hands. I walked to the dugout and went to the bucket where the batboy kept game balls for the ump. I reached in and fished a ball out of the bucket. I put it into my glove.

I'll pretend this is the game ball, I told myself. Nobody will ever know.

I never said anything to A-Rod about throwing my ball into the stands. I knew my place as a rookie. He probably just forgot it was my first big-league appearance. I had more important items on the agenda, anyway, such as staying in the big leagues, and for a fringe prospect, that was by no means a sure thing.

Chapter 12

MAJOR PROBLEMS

There's a flip side to the grouchy neighbor in the clubhouse story.

My first road trip took me to Toronto, home of the Blue Jays. Before a game, Jeff Brantley, veteran reliever and fellow Southeastern Conference guy (Mississippi State) invited me for lunch at a nearby mall. This suited me since I didn't get home before I was called up and had very few street clothes with me. I needed to shop.

At the store, I picked out a pair of slacks, two collared shirts, and a blazer. While I was trying things on, Jeff did his own shopping. When I emerged from the dressing room, he was at the register, signing a credit card receipt. Next to him were two large bags stuffed with clothes, shoes, belts—the works. All for me.

I glanced at the receipt. The total was more than $1,200. "What are you doing?" I asked.

"You needed a few clothes, so we got you a few clothes," he said. "I'm happy to help you out."

I tried to thank him, but he stopped me.

"You know how you can thank me? Someday you do it for a rookie," he said.

I made two more relief appearances over the next ten days, one good, one not so good. I was throwing pretty well, starting to believe that I could get big-league hitters out, trying to give in to the rhythms of big-league life, some parts of which are decidedly unsettling.

In the bathroom one day before a game, I saw something on the tile floor in one of the stalls. I looked closer.

It was a syringe.

My mind raced with thoughts about how and why it got there. Had this needle just injected a Texas Ranger with anabolic steroids? You could hazard a guess when you ran through the roster of my muscle-laden teammates. I'd never seen a syringe in a baseball clubhouse before. I've not seen one since. Maybe it was used for some legitimate medical purpose I didn't know about. But I couldn't shake the feeling that I was looking at a weapon somebody left at a crime scene.

I didn't tell anybody about the syringe. I wanted to believe my teammates were clean, though I had doubts. There's no denying the scope of the wreckage caused by needles during the so-called steroid era, and by all the feats illegal drug use helped produce. Performance-enhancing drugs hurt the game, and hurt me too. How many long balls hit by bulked-up juicers would've died on the track and gotten me out of an inning? How many balls muscled over the infield would've wound up in fielders' gloves? Nobody will ever know. I didn't stay up nights thinking about it, but I never forgot the sight of the syringe on the bathroom floor, either.

The bottom line for me on performance-enhancing drugs is simple: Guys who used them cheated. Cheated their opponents, their fans, and the game. But it's more personal than that: The guys who did it robbed me of the opportunity for fair play, because it wasn't just hitters who were using steroids. I'll never know how many guys were called up ahead of me, or kept their major-league careers alive, by using juice to add an extra five miles per hour to their fastball.

Just Say No to Steroids

Using steroids is not just unsportsmanlike. It's a terrible thing to do to your body. Yes, some players may have extended their careers by a few years, but the trade-offs are massive. Steroid use can cause acne, baldness, liver damage, increased aggressiveness (known as 'roid rage), breast development, and impotence in males. (That's right, guys. Steroids can make your testicles shrink.) People who stop using anabolic steroids also often suffer from depression. There are even cases of suicide linked to steroid withdrawal.

Why would anybody risk their life to hit a few more home runs, or pitch a few more innings in the bigs?

Right before our next series at home, manager Johnny Oates resigned. I was sorry to see him go. He was a man who was always willing to give an underdog a chance.

His replacement was Jerry Narron, an ex-catcher. I didn't know him well, so I hoped he had seen something in me he liked. That can be as important as anything. Baseball is a game of chance. Sometimes a ballplayer's promotion hinges on a coach looking his way when he rips a home run in spring training or throws a nasty fastball. The fates can be kind, and cruel. You can't dwell on it, either way.

On the final day of the series, our starter Darren Oliver was hit in his pitching hand in the first inning by a line drive drilled directly up the middle. Oliver's hand swelled immediately; his day was done almost before it began.

New manager Narron scanned his relievers and chose me to take over. I came in and got lit up like a gas can. Carlos Lee and Chris Singleton hit two-run doubles, and Lee and Paul Konerko hit back-to-back homers. In four and two-thirds, I surrendered seven hits and six runs for my first major-league defeat. It didn't improve my mood when I heard White Sox manager Jerry

Manuel in a postgame interview say they knew they had a good chance after Oliver got hurt because teams usually bring in one of their worst relievers in such a situation.

I filed that comment away. You never know when you might need some extra motivation.

With Oliver's injury, and me working long relief, the Rangers decided they needed a fresh arm from Oklahoma City for the rest of the week. Guess who got sent back down to make room? I can't say I was shocked. I didn't have a real high opinion of myself as a pitcher at that moment. Maybe they even picked up on that. After four appearances, twelve innings, and eighteen days, my first trip to the big leagues ended. I was sad, but not borderline homicidal, the way I was on the day of The Retraction.

I returned to Oklahoma City, to the apartment by the Dumpster, but all was not doom and gloom. God had given me a great gift: Anne was pregnant. I wound up having one of my best years, going 11-7 with a 3.75 ERA in a notorious hitters' league, using a fastball, a cutter, a changeup, and an occasional knuckleball—a pitch I'd messed around with for years, ever since Granddaddy told me that he threw it.

I expected to be called up to the big club again when the rosters expanded on September 1, but the call never came. That was a much bigger blow than being sent down in May. In September, clubs usually call up everybody who is remotely on the radar.

Sure enough, when I was back in Nashville at the end of the year, playing for the RedHawks against the Sounds, Lee Tunnell called me over—I was R.A. in this conversation, not Dewclaw—and told me the Rangers had taken me off the forty-man roster, leaving me unprotected, free to be picked up by any other team. Lee broke it to me as gently as he could. He knew what it meant.

We both knew.

It meant the Rangers thought I was worth about as much as a used resin bag. It meant, one month from my twenty-seventh birthday, I was looking at an extremely murky future.

Or none at all. At least, not in baseball

Money was (again) tight, and this time, there was a baby on the way, so I took a job in the off-season working for a physical therapist, doing ultrasound treatments on injured patients. I spent a lot of time trying to convince myself I was more than a 4A player.

A 4A player is a guy who excels at Triple-A, but can't cut it in the majors

It was not an easy argument to win.

The 2002 season started for me, again, in Oklahoma City. Six years after the draft, it was hard to see anything that resembled progress. When other RedHawks got the call-up that year, I found myself turning into one of those jealous types, resentful that I didn't get the call.

I didn't like where my career was going—or not going. I did a lot of praying about it, finally deciding that I needed to start thinking outside the baseball box. At twenty-seven, with my track record, the end could be imminent.

In the middle of the season, I called a friend, Trigg Wilkes, who ran camps for the YMCA along the east coast of Florida, to ask if he thought there was a job for me in his organization.

"Sure," Trigg said. "But I hope you aren't ready to pull the plug on baseball. You are still a young guy with a lot of potential."

I'm not sure if Trigg was being polite, or if he really believed that. I, myself, was having real doubts about my potential.

I finished 2002 with an 8-7 record and a 4.09 ERA. I gave up 176 hits in 154 innings, which, if not pitiful, was pretty darn lousy. I couldn't even call myself a 4A pitcher with those numbers.

Back in Nashville, I tried to be hopeful but felt mostly discouraged. I'd spent my whole life hearing country singers warbling about guys with dead-end jobs and hard-luck lives. I didn't want to be one of them. The YMCA was looking better all the time.

In the off-season, a Venezuelan team offered me $10,000 to play winter ball for them. I took it, unsure of how many more offers like this I'd ever get.

The Zulia Eagles played in the northwestern part of the country, a region that is home to Lake Maracaibo, one of the largest lakes in South America, as well as massive oil and gas reserves.

Venezuela was in turmoil when I arrived. The military had tried but failed to overthrow President Hugo Chávez earlier that year. At the US State Department's urging, I checked in with the US embassy. Its officials didn't sugarcoat the situation: "This is a dangerous place," they said. "You need to be careful at all times."

Protestors were out in force in the streets, as were

people wielding machine guns. I heard gunshots all the time.

Because I was a person who swam in lagoons with alligators, I braved the streets a few times to observe the commotion firsthand. I went to a bullfight and sampled the local cuisine, trying to assimilate into Zulia life.

What the protestors wanted was a new election. They didn't get it, but midway through the Eagles' schedule, they did succeed in shutting down the baseball season, the outbursts of violence making the idea of playing in—or attending—a baseball game too risky. A day after the season was officially canceled, the US embassy directed me to stay in my hotel until further notice. This time, I heeded their warning. I hunkered down, eating pizza with pork and pesto, the only available food option, for the next five days, reading and watching TV and looking out at the oil platforms in Lake Maracaibo.

People swarmed the airport, trying to leave the country as soon as possible, but I finally got a seat on a US-bound flight. The Eagles arranged a two-car escort to the airport, vehicles on either side of the one I was in. On the flight home, I decided that even though my chances to play professional baseball might soon dwindle, the ones that required bulletproof protection were offers I could refuse.

Shortly before the 2003 season, I got a phone call from the Rangers' newest manager, Buck Showalter. I'd never gotten a call from a manager in January before. My first thought was, "This is going to be bad news," but it would be tough to dent my happiness at the moment. I was cradling my baby daughter Gabriel in my arms when the phone rang.

Buck asked about my off-season and I skipped the part about dodging bullets in Zulia.

"I just wanted to let you know we're going to give you a good long look in camp this spring," Buck said. "I know you've kind of been swept under the rug and that you haven't always gotten a fair shot to show what you can do. But I think you have a lot to offer this organization, and you are going to get a chance to prove it."

There really weren't words adequate to describe how much I appreciated his calling me. "All I want to do is help the club," I told him. "I believe I can do that too."

I hung up so excited for spring training that I wished I could report that afternoon, but there was a month to go. I spent it going on long nighttime runs through the quiet streets of Green Hills, visualizing myself on the mound, getting big-league hitters out. I was in as good a shape as I'd ever been when I arrived in Port Charlotte in mid-February. The new manager had promised I was going to get a fair shot, and you can't ask for more than that.

R.A.'S TIPS FOR YOUNG PITCHERS

Run. *Most starting pitchers in the major leagues are great endurance athletes. Running not only helps you build stamina, but it's a fantastic way to work out any soreness you might be feeling from a previous throwing session. Fatigue is your enemy. Not only will it result in a poor pitching performance, it can also lead to injury. Most power pitchers will also tell you that—believe it or not—running helps their fastball, since so much of their power comes from their legs.*

Mom and me, age eight months, at Lipscomb University in 1974. It was my first baseball game.

Me at age one, in 1975.

Mom, Dad, and me, age three. My parents got divorced when I was eight.

My dad and me, age four, building a snowman.

My kindergarten picture from
Glencliff Elementary School, Nashville.

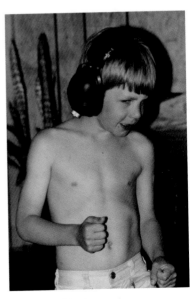

Me at age seven.

Me at age seven, playing in the instructional
(coach-pitch) league for the YMCA.
(Note the nice socks.)

Anne's brother, Bo, and me in 1988.

Trying to steal a kiss from my future bride in seventh grade.

Playing quarterback for Montgomery Bell Academy, Nashville, 1992.

LEFT: A picture from my senior year in high school, pitching for Montgomery Bell Academy.

BELOW: After the Tennessee state championship. *Left to right:* my stepmother, Susan; Dad; Grandma Dickey; my dad's cousin Dustin; me; my dad's cousin Randy; and Mom.

Anne and me when we started dating in 1993.

ABOVE: Anne and me after a University of Tennessee game in 1995.

RIGHT: Grandaddy and me after a University of Tennessee baseball game in the spring of 1996.

Kris Benson, R.A. Dickey, Braden Looper,
Seth Greisinger & Billy Koch (from left)
Lead Team USA Into Atlanta
BONUS SUMMER SHOPPER SECTION

I was thrilled to appear on the cover of *Baseball America* before the 1996 Olympic Games, with the four other U.S. starters. (*Left to right:* Kris Benson, me, Braden Looper, Seth Greisinger, and Billy Koch.) I was less thrilled when the photo—check out the bend in my elbow compared with the other guys'—prompted the Rangers to put me through tests that revealed the lack of an ulnar collateral ligament in my right elbow, costing me almost my entire $810,000 bonus.

(*Photo courtesy of Robert Gurganus,* Baseball America*)*

Second baseman Warren Morris and me after the U.S. men's baseball team received a bronze medal at the 1996 summer Olympics in Atlanta.

Anne Bartholomew and I were married in Nashville on December 13, 1997, before an intimate gathering of five hundred family and friends. *Left to right:* Anne's father, Sam Bartholomew; Anne's younger brother Will; Anne; me; Anne's youngest brother, Ben; Anne's mother, Vicki; and Bo.

With Anne's family. *Left to right:* Will; Will's wife, Shelly; Sam; Vicki; Ben; me; Anne; and Bo.

My mom and her brothers and sisters. *Left to right:* Lynn Caldwell, Mandy Bowers, Bob Bowers, Mom, Ricky Bowers, Helen Bowers, and Debbie Bowers. They all cared for me in some way.

LEFT: My good friend and fellow pitcher Jonathan Johnson and me in the Rangers bullpen during my first call-up in 2001.

RIGHT: My sister, Jane, and me with my daughter Gabriel, age one and a half, and Jane's daughter Abby, age nine.

At my first big-league game. *Left to right:* YMCA organizer Darlene Wilkes; Dad; my stepmom, Susan; Jennifer Binkley (Trig and Darlene's daughter); YMCA organizer Trigg Wilkes (Darlene's husband); Mom; Anne; Rob Merriman; Rob's wife, Denise; and my high school friend David Fitzgerald.

Anne and our son Eli in Seattle, in July 2008. I was playing for the Mariners then.

Phil Niekro and me in the winter of 2009. I drove to Atlanta to work with Phil on my knuckleball.

Mom and me at the beach in 2010.

Going underground:
Eli, Lila, and Gabriel join me for our first family outing on the New York City subway system, not long after I joined the Mets in 2010.

Teaching Prince Harry how to throw a knuckleball.

Anne and me as we celebrate our fourteenth anniversary on December 13, 2011.

Introducing Van Allen Dickey.

Eli and me at the beach, fall 2010.

Cuddling with my girls: Gabriel is on my right and Lila on my left.

Darth Vader Senior (me)
and Darth Vader Junior (Eli)
get primed for Halloween.

Eli and I figure it's time to start teaching
Van the wonder of words.

Van's probably not sure what
to make of me or my
Darth Vader costume.

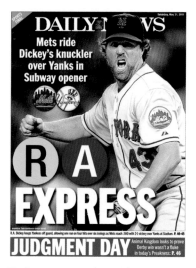

Pitching against the Yankees in New York is always a special event.

(Photo courtesy of New York Daily News)

Battling the Marlins at Citi Field.

(Photo courtesy of New York Daily News/Robert Sabo)

Me, in the dugout after losing my no-hit bid against the Phillies.

(Photo courtesy of New York Daily News/ Howard Simmons)

	1	2	3	4	5	6	7	8	9	R	H	E	BALLS	STRIKES	OUTS
PIRATES	0	2	0	1	0	0	0	0	2	5	9	0	0	0	0
Mets	0	1	0	1	4	0	0	0	X	6	8	0			

The scoreboard at Citi Field after I got my 20th win of the 2012 season. I threw 128 pitches to get the win, helped by David Wright's 3-run home run in the 5th inning.

(Photo courtesy of Jim McIsaac/Getty Images Sport/Getty Images)

Closer to home, at the DeKalb County Fairgrounds, Alexandria, Tennessee, June 2011. *Left to right:* Eli, me, Van, Gabriel, Anne, and Lila. *(Photo courtesy of Mark Tucker)*

Chapter 13

FUNERAL FOR MY FASTBALL

Early in the 2005 season, I landed on the disabled list, prompting a meeting in manager Buck Showalter's office. Orel Hershiser, now an ESPN analyst but back then the Rangers' pitching coach, did most of the talking.

I was scared that what they planned to tell me was that I had run out of road. It was now nine years since the Rangers drafted me. I'd been on the big-league roster in 2003 and 2004 as a spot starter and long reliever, my first extended time in the big leagues.

Orel Hershiser knows a lot about pitching. He won the 1988 Cy Young Award by putting together one of the best seasons in history, winning twenty-three games for the Dodgers, a performance that included a streak of fifty-nine consecutive scoreless innings pitched. He is also a good man, one whom I trusted. He got right to the point.

"After you finish rehabbing your shoulder, what would

you think about going back to Oklahoma City to learn how to become a full-time knuckleball pitcher?" Orel asked. "I'm sure you don't want to go back to the minors, but we think it's your best chance for success. You have a good knuckleball already. You have the perfect makeup to make it work, because you know how to compete and we know how hard you'll go after it."

Orel and I had talked about this before. I'd done bullpen sessions for him in which I threw nothing but the knuckleball, a pitch I used very occasionally.

He'd always been positive and supportive, which was exactly what I needed at the moment because I was full of doubt and short on hope, a thirty-year-old veteran whose career hung by the frayed leather string that holds a glove together. I'd never been a guy to obsess about stats, but I could not run from my numbers. Over parts of four big-league seasons, I had pitched in seventy-two games, amassing a 15-17 win-loss record and a 5.48 ERA. I'd given up 293 hits in 239⅔ innings.

Those are ugly numbers.

Later, Mark "Goose" Connor, our bullpen coach, confirmed for me just how shaky my situation was.

"They aren't going to bring you back to the big leagues as a conventional pitcher, R.A.," he said. "You're going to come back as a knuckleball pitcher or you're not going to come back at all."

What they were telling me was that it was over for my fastball. The death knell had sounded. It was hard to wrap my mind around that. Okay, so not many people had ever confused me with Nolan Ryan. I got that. But I'd always been able to throw a hard sinking fastball at 92 or 93 miles per hour. I became an All-American, an Olympian, and a first-round draft choice because I had a big-league fastball and a big-league changeup to play off it.

Now I was supposed to say good-bye to all that and join the ranks of Hoyt Wilhelm, the Niekro brothers, and Charlie Hough?

That's exactly what they were asking me to do, because radar guns don't lie, and all spring, my fastball had been topping out at 85 or 86 mph.

I wanted to run from the truth, escape, the same way I did when I slept in empty houses. But in my heart I knew what was going on.

My arm was spent.

Bleakness swept over me. Anne and I had two little girls by this point. (Our daughter Lila Anne was born in June 2003.) I had no backup plan if the Rangers let me go. No family business. No standing job offer. Nothing. Worse, I had lost all belief in my ability to get big-league hitters out. I'd get the call in the pen and feel as if I was going into battle using a peashooter against guys carrying bazookas.

I felt overmatched, like the first time I took the entrance exam for Montgomery Bell Academy. I dreaded going to work. Baseball wasn't fun anymore.

So I looked at Buck and Orel and told them: "I'll do it. I'll go to Oklahoma City. I'll become a full-time knuckleball pitcher and I promise you I'll give it everything I've got."

I stood and shook hands with them, a life-changing, seven-minute meeting complete.

I felt as if a weight had been lifted, as if they had thrown me a lifeline. Lightness doesn't come easily to me, but I walked out of there feeling almost buoyant. I was reminded of a quote from Romans 5:3–4 in the New Testament: "We rejoice in our sufferings, knowing that suffering produces endurance, and endurance produces character, and character produces hope."

Hope is good.

I Googled every knuckleballer I could think of. I wasn't looking for tips. I needed to know how many games they won after turning thirty years old. A few clicks yielded the astounding truth:

Phil Niekro won 287 games after the age of thirty.

Charlie Hough won 182.

Phil's brother, Joe, won 163. Tom Candiotti, 122. Wilbur Wood, 105.

Tim Wakefield had 156 (so far) and was still going strong.

Add them all up, and the best knuckleballers of the last few decades had won over one thousand games in their thirties and beyond. It is one of the best perks about life in the knuckle world: Because you don't throw the ball hard and you do no twisting or contorting, the pitch puts almost no strain on your arm. It enables you to not only eat innings but inhale them.

The same week that Buck and Orel redirected my future, Tim Wakefield dominated the Yankees twice in five days. Not that I needed more convincing, but still.

So I left behind my career as a conventional pitcher with the paltry fifteen victories and the laughable 5.48 ERA. Who cares about throwing 90 miles per hour? I was tired of being average, or worse. Tired of being in the margins on the Texas Rangers' roster. I had no idea how this experiment was going to go, but I was ready to find out.

Chapter 14

KNUCKLING UNDER

Throwing a baseball slow is hard.

After thousands of pitches in the 90 mile per hour range, I was now trying to float them across the plate in the low 60s. It was like trading in a sports car for a tricycle.

I had nobody to help me figure out how to do it correctly. Lee Tunnell, my pitching coach, would have given his own arm to help me if he could. But like almost everybody else in baseball, he didn't know anything about the knuckleball.

So I did my own research, going up and down the bench, interviewing hitters: Have you ever faced a knuckleball pitcher? What was hard about it? What was easy about it? I started with Adrian Gonzalez, a kid first baseman and future superstar.

"I hate hitting against knuckleball pitchers," he admitted. "It messes up your balance, timing, everything."

Next up: Ian Kinsler, another star-in-waiting. "It's no fun because every knuckleball is different," he said.

The responses gave me hope, because every hitter who had ever faced a knuckleball thought they were a pain in the butt to hit. I can do this, I told myself. I can make this pitch work for me. This was my new reality: *I am a knuckleball pitcher. I am committed to being a knuckleball pitcher.*

This was my last chance. I could not screw up my last chance.

My first start as a full-time knuckleballer was against the Iowa Cubs in Bricktown, the home ballpark of the RedHawks. I had spent parts of six years in Oklahoma City. I knew the names of the vendors and the cleanup crew, was good friends with the cops, and had logged more miles up and down Mickey Mantle Drive, the main road outside the park, than any other RedHawk. I owned more official team records too, none of which I was in a rush to add to, because I didn't want to be there long enough to do so.

An hour before first pitch, I ducked into a little room between the players' lounge and the kitchen.

On my knees, I prayed. I didn't pray for a no-hitter or a shutout, or for the best knuckleball since Phil Niekro no-hit the Padres in 1973. That would be tantamount to me choosing the outcome I wanted and asking God to make it happen.

I prayed for the strength and courage to stay the course and do my best, and to trust in God's will for me, no matter what the outcome.

The night turned out to be an excellent test of my trust, because I was horrible. The game resembled one long batting practice for the Cubs. Line drives rained down around me. Our outfielders ran as if it were the Olympic trials, doing wind sprints to the wall in pursuit of knuckleballs that didn't knuckle. Just before the Cubs' run total hit double figures, I paused on the mound in the midst of the carnage.

I rubbed up the ball. I looked to the horizon. I felt wretched. So wretched, I thought I might vomit right there on the mound—the same disgust I felt in the Olympic bullpen when we were getting clubbed by Japan in 1996. I knew there would be a learning curve, but did I ever expect this?

No, I did not.

When my manager, Bobby Jones, finally took me out, my pitching line was five and two-thirds innings, fourteen hits, twelve earned runs, five walks, no strikeouts. I left the field serenaded by a hearty chorus of boos, all of them richly deserved. When Bobby got back to the dugout, he said, "You're getting the ball again in five days."

"I'll be ready," I told him.

I went to the movies after the game to forget what happened. Fat chance. I ate popcorn in the dark by myself—I don't even remember the movie—and told myself again about how important it was to embrace this experiment. I was fighting for my professional baseball life. What could I learn from this disaster and do better next time?

I still had no knuckleball coach and no clue, but somehow I did get better. The next start, I gave up six hits and four runs. I wound up winning seven of my last eight decisions. I was still not very good, but I was light-years better than I was against the Iowa Cubs. The Rangers called me up in September for a start against the Orioles.

I was petrified.

Could I really face major-league hitters throwing a ball 60 or 70 miles per hour? All I thought about was survival, how I could get through it. I scanned the Orioles roster for their most dangerous hitters, guys like Miguel Tejada and Jay Gibbons. In the film room,

Orel and I studied a video of Tim Wakefield pitching against the Orioles. I said a prayer, but I was not sure that would be enough.

The Orioles' leadoff hitter, Bernie Castro, hit a line-drive single to start the first. Melvin Mora, the number two hitter, followed with another single.

Two batters. Two hits.

Too much stress.

Then I walked Tejada. Three minutes into the game, I had a bases-loaded, nobody-out catastrophe on my hands.

Was this going to be the Iowa Cubs all over again? Could I handle another body blow like that game?

Jay Gibbons stepped into the batter's box. I forced myself to battle. I fell behind, two and one, but I refused to give in, and Gibbons grounded into a double play on the next pitch. Two runs scored, but I lived to face another batter. In fact, I lasted until the seventh, giving up only five hits overall. At this stage of my knuckleballing career, I would take those results every time. Orel congratulated me as I came off the mound.

I was the most relieved man in Texas.

A day later, I got a more comprehensive review. "We want you to approach this more like Tim Wakefield,"

Orel said. "Throw more knuckleballs, and throw them slower."

About 65 percent of my pitches against the Orioles were knuckleballs. Orel wanted that number at 80 percent or higher.

"Your future is with the knuckleball. You've got to throw it more," he said.

The Rangers organization had been good to me. Orel had been good to me. I wanted to please them, so I would do as they asked, even though I felt lost. I had no real feel or command for the pitch I was throwing.

I faced the Mariners in my second start, committed to following Orel's instructions. Fear dominated my emotions. I was in a throw-the-ball-and-hope-for-the-best place. I hate that place. I had always been a fighter. I take pride in being a fighter. From the time scouts started looking at me when I was in high school, I always got high marks for being a competitor who would go at the opposition with all I had. I could grind out victories even when I didn't have my best stuff.

Now? I stood on the mound thinking I was not good enough.

I tried talking myself into believing I was the same guy I was at Tennessee—the exact conversation I had with myself in 1996, when I first reported to the

Rangers' minor-league camp. Remember the pitcher who threw 183 pitches to get his team into the College World Series, who threatened to fight the coach when he tried to take him out? That is who you are, I told myself.

Right. I felt like the shadow of that guy.

Somehow I got the victory against the Mariners, even though I gave up six hits and six runs in five-plus innings. I stumbled to the end of the season with little idea of where the ball was going. I put up very shaky numbers. The transition to becoming a knuckleball pitcher now seemed like a very bad idea.

Then I met Charlie.

Chapter 15

THE JEDI COUNCIL OF KNUCKLEBALLERS

Part One: The Sheriff of Knuckleball County

I met Charlie Hough for the first time in the visitors' locker room at Angel Stadium in Anaheim, California. Charlie looks—then and now—more like the grizzled lawman in an old Western than a former major-league pitcher. But Charlie had what I was after: expertise. He pitched twenty-five seasons in the big leagues and won 162 games after the age of thirty-four.

Meeting Charlie Hough, for me, was like meeting Cy Young himself.

Like a hyped-up toddler, I peppered Charlie with questions within minutes of shaking his hand. The subject, of course, was baseball's most mysterious pitch.

It is a pitch, I was learning, that is as hard to throw consistently as it is to catch.

The Rangers wanted Charlie to assess my chances for succeeding as a knuckleballer. I wanted him to teach me everything he knew. I looked at his weathered face and thought: This is probably how it feels to talk about the Bible with the Pope.

Charlie wanted to see me throw, so we made our way to the field, the sensei and the student. I was nervous.

What if Charlie told the Rangers my knuckleball stunk? What if he told them that the idea of reinventing R. A. Dickey, long-ago phenom, into a flutterballer was going nowhere?

I hate my insecurities. I tried to ignore them.

Hough became a knuckleballer after injuring his arm in the minor leagues. He learned to throw it in a day, but it took most of his career to be able to throw it for strikes. And that's the key. The best knuckleball in the world is worthless if you can't get it over the plate.

"How do you learn to control it?" I asked.

"You throw it and you keep throwing it. You throw it every day," Charlie said. "You find guys to catch you. You throw it against outfield walls. You throw it against alley walls. You keep at it. It takes time and it takes patience to get the feel for it and to master it, and even after you think you have, you better have a real thick skin if you are going to be a knuckleball pitcher."

"Why is that?" I asked.

"Because you are going to have games when you throw five wild pitches or give up four home runs—games when you just don't have it," Charlie said. "Every pitcher is going to have games when he doesn't have it, even Hall of Fame pitchers. The difference is that when you have an ugly game as a knuckleball pitcher, it's really ugly. It's going to happen, I promise you. You have to keep faith in yourself and your pitch, even if everybody else loses faith."

In the bullpen, I anxiously threw a dozen knuckleballs for Charlie. He wanted to see my grip, and I held the ball up with the fingernails of my index and middle fingers biting into the runway, the part of the ball where the seams come closest together. He suggested I move my nails to just underneath the horseshoe, the part of the baseball where the seams form an upside-down, U-shaped curve. It's a small change but actually a completely different grip.

"It's a better way to kill the spin," Charlie said.

I threw a pitch with his grip. It felt weird. I kept throwing. The weirdness didn't lift—not that day, not for days and weeks afterward—but I stayed with it.

I never threw a ball with my old grip again.

From that day forward, I never took to the mound without thinking about staying inside the doorframe, either.

Charlie is big on visuals, and the doorframe is the best of them. After watching my delivery, with an overhead windup and arms and legs extending in various directions, Charlie told me to imagine a doorway, and to pitch so that all of my movements, and limbs, could fit within that opening.

"If you're flying all over—if your hand is hitting the side of the imaginary doorframe—what's going to happen?" he asked. "The ball will be more likely to spin. Spin is the enemy, especially backward spin. You want to simplify things. You want fewer moving pieces and to have all those pieces moving forward toward the plate."

"Why is spin so bad?" I wondered.

"Because knuckleballs that spin are the ones you don't get back," Charlie said. "Maybe you can get away with a little forward spin, but backward spin? Forget it.

Those are the ones that sit up. Those are the ones that wind up way back in the seats."

So I worked on controlling my limbs, staying inside the imaginary doorway. I threw for Charlie on successive days. After about a hundred pitches on the second day, Charlie told me to stop. By this point, I was drenched in sweat and doubt. I didn't have any feel for how I'd done. Charlie is a jolly, affable man, but he's also totally old-school, not one to go overboard with compliments.

I screwed up my courage to ask him straight-out, "Do you think I can do this?"

He gave me a tight little smile. "I think you have a chance," he said.

My first throwing session with Charlie convinced me I needed to spend more time with him. Twice that off-season, I went to see him at his home in California. I threw a lot of knuckleballs, but I wasn't stressing my arm because I wasn't trying to throw them with maximum velocity. "Pitch count should never be an issue for you again," Charlie said.

New grip. Doorframe. I felt a glimmer of hope. "How do I know when I've thrown a good one?" I asked.

"You'll know by how it comes out of your hand," Charlie said. "You'll know in that instant. You won't need to see it cross the plate or see a batter swing."

"If the knuckleball is so effective, how come so few people throw it?" I asked.

"Because it takes a lot of patience to learn how to throw it for strikes," he said. "More patience than most people have."

Ten thousand? Twenty thousand? Fifty thousand? I threw a lot of knuckleballs that winter, most of them against a white cinder-block wall in the gym of the Ensworth School in Nashville, where Uncle Ricky was the athletic director. I didn't want a catcher. I just wanted the wall and my bucket of balls. I started at forty feet from the wall, then back up to fifty feet, then sixty. I threw almost every day, for up to an hour. Some days were better than others. On the bad days, it felt like I was hurling a hunk of volcanic rock. On the bad days, the sound of my screams bounced off the gym walls.

I kept throwing, thinking of Larry Bird in his number 33 Boston Celtics uniform. Bird did an interview once where he talked about never letting himself be outworked, about being haunted by a fear that somebody, somewhere, was taking shots while he was resting.

Nobody was going to outwork me, either. Maybe I wouldn't make it as a big-league knuckleballer, but it wouldn't be from lack of effort. I kept throwing, picking out a particular cinder block to hit each time, knowing that whatever happened, I could at least comfort myself with the knowledge that I did the work.

When I left the gym, I drove around Nashville with only my left hand on the wheel so I could practice my knuckleball grip with my right. When I drove our daughter Gabriel to nursery school, the ball was in my right hand. When I ran out to get diapers or go to the bank, the ball was in my right hand.

There was another tip from Charlie: There's no substitute for having the ball in your hand. I still keep a baseball in my car. You never stop working on your grip.

I returned to Charlie's for a refresher course in early February, right before reporting to Arizona for spring training. I certainly wasn't sure I could make the Rangers' roster in 2006 or if my knuckleball was good enough to get big-league hitters out, but I knew it was better than it was at the end of 2005.

I showed up early for spring training, riding my bike to the park and eating most of my meals at Arby's to save money. Every day I filled up a five-gallon bucket with baseballs and threw knuckleballs into the netting of the batting cage. After I'd warmed up, I'd corral Andy Hawkins, a former big-league pitcher and our Triple-A pitching coach, and throw another three or four dozen knucklers to him.

After a few weeks, I noticed he wasn't catching the ball as often. I was hitting him in the knee, the groin, the stomach.

"I'm going to have to start wearing armor," he complained, smiling.

I'd never been happier about hurting someone.

I started a game against the Japanese national team, which was getting ready for the World Baseball Classic. I pitched well and struck out Ichiro Suzuki twice. In another start, I shut down the Cubs for five innings. When I started throwing the knuckleball, I threw maybe two good ones out of ten. Now it was closer to five or six good ones out of ten.

One afternoon, after throwing on a back field at the Rangers complex, I hitched a ride back to the clubhouse on a golf cart with Goose Connor, who had replaced Orel Hershiser as pitching coach. Like Charlie, Goose is not the type to gush or give pep talks. His encouragement is much more measured.

"Keep doing what you're doing," Goose said.

The Rangers of that era were not known for pitching. They were known for having a completely stacked lineup that didn't give opposing pitchers much of a chance to work around dangerous hitters. One of the projected starters, Adam Eaton, got hurt in spring training, meaning there was at least one spot in the starting rotation that Buck and Goose had to fill.

My anxiety about making the club built each day. The thought of going back to the RedHawks for a seventh season, and hearing chatter about running for mayor, was not appealing. I prayed for calmness and for the strength to keep working on my craft.

I was at my locker one afternoon in late March when a clubhouse guy told me, "Buck wants to see you in his office."

The moment of truth had arrived. Was I a big leaguer again?

Buck and Goose were waiting for me in Buck's office in the clubhouse. I tried to read their faces as I walked in, but they didn't give anything away. That's okay, because Buck didn't draw things out.

"Congratulations, R.A.," he said. "You've worked your tail off and you've made the club. You're going to be in the rotation."

I paused a minute to let it sink in. I wasn't stunned,

R.A.'S TIPS FOR YOUNG PITCHERS

How to Throw a Knuckleball

The knuckleball is the only pitch in baseball that works by doing nothing. Curveballs curve. Cutters cut. Sinkers sink. You want your knuckleball to float to the plate, rotation-free, and let the laws of physics take it from there, the ball wobbling and wiggling and shimmying and shaking. Or not. Sometimes the knuckleball will be unhittable and sometimes it will be uncatchable, but rarely is it predictable. It's one of the first things you have to accept as a knuckleballer: The pitch has a mind of its own.

1. *Grip the ball under the "horseshoe" seam with the nails of your pointer and middle fingers. Dig your nails right into the leather.*
2. *Using your thumb and index fingers as stability points, cock*

but it was still the best possible news I could've received.

I shook their hands, and floated back across the clubhouse. I called Anne and then I called the man who made it all possible.

Charlie Hough.

"Woo-hoo," Charlie said when I told him I'd be starting the fourth game of the year, against the Detroit Tigers. "Woo-hoo" is Charlie's highest praise.

your wrist back to a 90-degree angle, or as close to it as possible.

3. *Wind up and release the ball with your momentum going through Charlie's "door-frame." Your hips should be almost square to the plate. This is the part that takes practice, but when you get it right, you'll throw a spinless ball that will wiggle and wobble and be really tough to hit.*

Whenever I threw a good knuckleball in front of him, that's what he said: "Woo-hoo."

It was not only a new season. It was a fresh start, a whole new career.

I said a prayer of thanks and counted the days till my start.

Chapter 16

THE WORST NIGHT OF MY LIFE

At 3:45 p.m. on April 6, 2006, I left my hotel, hopped on my bike, and pedaled to the ballpark for the most important start of my baseball life.

There was no other way to think about it. If I wanted to stay in professional baseball, I had to be able to get big-league hitters out with my knuckleball. I would leave my fastball and changeup on a shelf in my locker. This was the night I became a full-fledged knuckler.

In the video room, I watched a tape of Wakefield pitching against the Tigers the year before, looking for reassurance that major-league hitters can be retired with the knuckleball. I needed convincing because I lacked confidence in myself.

I didn't really want to send R. A. Dickey out there against the Tigers. I wanted to send out Tim Wakefield.

I said a prayer before heading to the outfield with bullpen catcher Josh Frasier. I started throwing and I had a pretty good knuckler on flat ground. We moved on to the bullpen mound, and it was even better, the ball fluttering, my confidence building to unaccustomed levels.

Over the PA, the lineup was announced. Game time. I prayed for confidence and for the courage to go after each Tiger in the batter's box.

Brandon Inge, the Tigers' third baseman, led off the first. I threw him a knuckleball for a strike to start the game. I wound up and delivered the 0-1 pitch, a knuckler that tumbled slowly toward the inner part of the plate. Rotation is my mortal enemy. As the ball approached the plate, Inge's eyes grew wide.

He put serious wood on it, driving the ball deep to left. I followed the flight of the ball, watching as it sailed over the fence.

Two pitches into the game, I was already down a run. Not the start I had in mind. At all.

I got the next two guys, and then Magglio Ordóñez stepped in. On a 1-0 pitch, I floated another knuckleball. He uncoiled on it. A loud *thwack* filled the park, followed by another ball disappearing over the left-field wall. The score was 2–0 and the Tigers' batting average against me in my knuckleball debut was .500.

Even in that moment I knew why. I prayed for confidence because I didn't have any. Once real live hitters appeared at the plate, I turned into a completely different pitcher than I was in the pen. I was tentative, afraid to make a mistake. I wasn't going after the Tigers' hitters, I was pitching scared. The upshot was that my knuckleballs weren't confounding the Tigers, they were coming into the plate looking like beach balls.

I got Dmitri Young to ground out to end the inning. In the dugout, Goose reminded me that plenty of pitchers get roughed up early on before settling into their rhythm.

"Just keep battling," he said.

We didn't score in the bottom of the first. The first Tigers' hitter in the top of the second was Chris Shelton, a power-hitting first baseman. Ahead 1-2, I threw another knuckler that sat up. Shelton took a huge slugger's cut at it and an instant later the ball was in orbit, another knuckler leaving the premises—quickly. If you're keeping score at home, that's 1,200 feet worth of dingers so far. And we were only in the top of the second inning.

Shelton wasn't three steps out of the box when I asked the umpire for a new ball. I had no intention of watching him round the bases. Instead, I rubbed up the ball, looking vacantly toward the sky, trying to fathom what was happening. I saw the blank faces of my infielders, shortstop Michael Young and first baseman Mark Teixeira, and thought how I was letting them down, letting the whole team down. The infield was as quiet as a library.

Get the next hitter, I scolded myself. This can still be a quality start if you stop it right here.

I retired the next three guys and managed to get through a bumpy third inning, despite a long fly and two line drives. It wasn't pretty, but it was scoreless, and that constituted progress. The first batter in the fourth was Dmitri Young. I struck him out, my first strikeout of the night.

Then it was Shelton's turn again. I went up on him, 1-2, just as I had the last time.

Don't make the same mistake, I reminded myself. If you miss, make sure you miss down. If you get Shelton, you'll be an out away from a second straight scoreless inning. There was still hope of salvaging this start.

Except that on my next pitch, I delivered another beach ball up in the zone. Shelton crushed it to left, way over the fence, farther than any of the others.

Goose paid a visit to the mound. He looked like an undertaker, only sadder.

"Let's just take a breath right now, okay?" he said. "Just keep fighting. Don't fold up. Take a breath and give us some innings."

Goose was right in everything he said. I took the breath. I told myself I was going to stop the carnage right there. The next hitter was Carlos Guillen, the shortstop. I walked him, bringing up center fielder Craig Monroe, who swung at the first pitch, one more knuckleball that did nothing. Monroe hit it halfway to El Paso. Now the score was 6–0, a full-blown debacle. I could take breaths until the 162nd game and it wasn't going to change the hideous truth: The biggest start of my life had turned into the worst start of my life.

Up next: Marcus Thames, the left fielder. No matter what, I was not going to let him hit a knuckleball out of the park.

Instead, I threw a fastball. And he hit that out of the park. My sixty-first, and last, pitch of the night.

As Thames circled the bases, I looked up into the half-filled stands and listened to boos rain down on me. It's hard to get baseball fans in Texas to boo you, but I did it, tying the modern record for most home runs given up in a start. My line was three and a third innings, eight hits, and seven runs. Buck came out to get me. The whole scene was completely surreal, as if I were at the center of a slow-motion highlight reel, Tigers swinging, Tigers slugging, balls flying out of the park, a home-run derby come to life. It seemed as if it took Buck a half hour to get to the mound.

I waited, feeling completely alone. It struck me as a very familiar feeling.

How long had I felt alone, bobbing and weaving through life, keeping people at a distance, terrified they'd get too close?

In a strange way, as I waited to hand Buck the ball and get out of there before any more Tigers could take me over the wall, I realized that was how I'd pitched that night, spending my three and a third innings doing the same sort of bobbing and weaving. I'd pitched with conviction during my warm-up. I'd thrown good knuckleballs, knuckleballs that had big movement, late movement, the kind that could make even the best hitters look silly.

And then the game started, and I hid. I pitched with fear, pitched like a wimp, doubting whether I was good enough to beat the Detroit Tigers and letting that doubt rob me of any shot I had at succeeding. As I let each pitch go that night, I had voices in my head saying, Please, let it be a strike, and, Please, don't let them hit it.

It was no way to pitch.

It was no way to live.

As I left the mound, I took in the scene: the anger of the fans; the little white lights telling the hideous truth on the scoreboard; the grim reality that I was indeed a marginal big-league pitcher. I wanted to believe that God had better things in store for me, and that this was not how my baseball life would end. I left The Ballpark the way I arrived, pedaling through the darkness as fast as I could, getting out of Dodge before any more baseballs could fly over the fence.

R.A.'S TIPS FOR YOUNG PITCHERS

Be cool. *Whether you have given up twenty runs or struck out twenty batters, don't be emotional on the mound. Be as steady as you can possibly be. Your opponents can read body language and they'll take advantage if they think the pressure is getting to you. An observer shouldn't be able to tell if you are throwing a no-hitter or are getting rocked. Save the emotion for the end of the game. Then you can celebrate or vent, whichever is called for.*

Chapter 17

REACHING BOTTOM

Baseball has records for everything. I'm pretty sure I own the record for shortest-lived happiness to start a season. How could it get any shorter? One minute I was thrilled to be in the Rangers' rotation, beginning what I hoped would be my successful second career, as a knuckleballer. The next I found myself joining my fellow knuckleballer Tim Wakefield in long-ball lore, giving up a record six home runs in one outing.

One minute Anne was in town to celebrate my reinvention, and to find a nice rental home for the season. The next I was thinking we might not need a house in Texas after all.

Sleep did not come easily that night. I opened the curtains to a perfect new Texas day, the sky deep blue, reminding myself it was only one game. I said out loud, for Anne and myself, "Let's remember, God's mercies are new every morning."

I had barely finished with "Amen" when a white

Hummer pulled into the hotel parking lot. A strapping young man got out of the car. When he turned around, I recognized him immediately: Rick Bauer.

I had met him in spring training. He was a former Orioles draft pick whom the Rangers signed after the 2005 season. He was slated to start the season in Oklahoma City. Now he was checking in to the Hyatt. You don't have to be a rocket scientist to connect the dots. Bauer, a six-foot-six-inch right-hander, had arrived to join the big club, which meant that somebody would be leaving the big club.

I was pretty sure that somebody was going to be me.

A shiny new Hummer delivering my shiny new replacement. Not exactly the answer I was seeking to my prayer.

When I got to the clubhouse, Buck called me in to his office, and closed the door. Buck had always supported me. I knew he didn't want to be doing this. But business is business.

"We had to use a lot of arms last night and we're short," he said. "We're going to send you to Oklahoma City."

I didn't say anything for a minute, for good reason. I was crushed.

This would be my seventh season in Oklahoma City, a place I associate totally with my mediocrity as a pitcher. I already owned all the RedHawk pitching records. Was this going to be the top line of my baseball résumé: a RedHawk immortal? Was this how it would end for me: Another sad-eyed prospect playing out the string on the prairie in front of a thousand fans and a mascot?

It's not quite how I envisioned it as a kid.

Of course, I was brutal the night before. Nobody had to tell me that. I just never thought I'd get only one start to prove myself.

One start! Who was I kidding? I'd been with the Rangers for a decade.

My next thought was: I may have worn a Rangers uniform for the last time.

I had to work to keep it together. With as much steel in my voice as I could muster, I stood and looked squarely at Buck. "I understand why you are doing this, but I just want to tell you one thing: That outing last night will not define me as a big-league pitcher. It won't. I can promise you that." My voice cracked midway through my speech.

We shook hands and I went to my locker to throw my stuff in a bag. I scanned the room, wondering if I'd ever be in a big-league clubhouse again.

Anne flew home so I could take the car to Oklahoma City. She wanted to come with me, but I was bad company. I wanted to brood. I drove north on Interstate 35, out of Texas and the big leagues, a stretch of road I knew far too well. I crossed into Oklahoma, passing through a town called Slaughterville.

Slaughterville. How perfect. I had been there the previous night, getting butchered by the Detroit Tigers.

It's a place I never wanted to visit again.

Two days after I returned to Oklahoma City, the Rangers took me off the forty-man roster again. In baseball-speak, this is called "designated for assignment," or DFA. In plain speech, it meant my value to the team was at the used rosin bag level again.

The Rangers figured there was no risk of losing me, because—let's face it—what was the market for a thirty-one-year-old knuckleballer who had just given up six home runs in one game? And the Rangers were right. Not a single club in the major leagues expressed any interest in my services. So I stayed in the RedHawks' rotation, and performed miserably. Through my first eight starts, my record was 2-5 and my ERA was over 7.00.

This switch to knuckleballing was supposed to make things better, not worse.

I had so many questions, so many worries. Baseball was only one of them. Anne was pregnant with our third child that summer. It should've been a joyful time, with our two healthy girls and a baby boy on the way, but how was I going to provide for my growing family? We'd just bought a house in Nashville; Anne and the kids stayed there so we didn't have to rent another house in Oklahoma City. I didn't even rent an apartment for myself. I stayed with a pastor friend, or at the Red Roof Inn, or at an Econo Lodge for seventy dollars a night. When the team went on the road, I checked out of the hotel and hauled my stuff to the clubhouse, then dragged it back to the hotel when we returned.

Between mounting financial pressure on one side and mounting baseball pressure on the other, I felt like Luke Skywalker, Chewbacca, Han Solo, and Princess Leia from *Star Wars: Episode IV* when they fall into a trash compactor and the walls start closing in on them. It felt as if all this trash was getting squeezed right up in my face.

Those feelings overpowered my wobbly faith. I resorted to my timeworn strategy: Escape. I lost myself in books, and movies, sitting in the back eating pop-corn. Playing baseball for a living is an escape itself. It is a life that can make you a spoiled kid, where your needs and whims are catered to, and selfishness is as prevalent as sunflower seeds.

People see the glamour and the big money of being a ballplayer, but they may not see the profound stress it puts on families. You're away for six weeks in spring training, and then you flit in and out of your family's life for the next six months. You say "good-bye" more than any other word, and even if you try to be a dedi-cated family man, you invariably miss things. Hugely important things. When our daughter Lila was born, I was in the Dallas/Fort Worth International Airport, trying to get a flight home. When our first son was born, I was in the visitors' clubhouse in Round Rock, Texas, right before a start, my mother-in-law holding up the phone as Elijah entered the world.

When you are away so much, almost every conversa-tion back home seems to be conducted in a pressure cooker, where you talk about new tires for the car, kids' ear infections, and the swelling cell phone bill.

If you have any self-awareness, you realize how uneven the distribution of responsibilities is. Your wife is checking for monsters under the bed in the middle of the night, and then getting up first thing to get the kids ready for school, while you are hanging with the guys after a game and sleeping until almost noon.

I felt guilt about this, and I felt inadequate in every way possible: in my walk with God, and especially in my role as husband and father.

I knew, more unconsciously than consciously, that the path I was on was not leading toward success in any aspect of my life. I knew part of the problem was my own, deep-seated fear that I was unworthy, which had been hanging around since the summer I was eight years old. More than a decade since the draft, I still could not shake the judgment that I was damaged, not because of my missing UCL, but because I had not been honest about who I was.

I was having a difficult year on the mound, and an even worse one in my marriage. Every time Anne and I talked, we argued.

Before the season even ended, she did the right thing: She kicked me out.

This was a whole lot worse than giving up six home runs in three and a third innings. I was on my way to becoming a father who could see his kids only on Tuesdays, Thursdays, and every other weekend.

My heart wasn't in baseball, but we needed the paycheck. I finished the RedHawks season with a 9-8 record and a 4.92 ERA, the sort of numbers that get you released.

I had never felt more lost.

Chapter 18

A LIFELINE

When the season ended, I returned to Nashville and moved into an empty house. We had bought a new one, where Anne and the kids were living, but the old one hadn't sold. That was home for me for the time being.

I did a lot of staring out the window, taking inventory of my sorry life. My self-esteem was so low, it didn't have a reading. God had blessed me with health and intelligence and a beautiful family, and look what I'd done with those gifts. Career minor leaguer with a bleak outlook for future success, absent father, lousy husband. I'd turned my life into a hopeless tangle of problems.

My goal was to win back my family. But I was beating up on myself so hard that the toxic voice inside was drowning out everything else: You are a failure. You wrapped your entire identity up in being a major-league pitcher and fell apart as a human being when you couldn't cut it. You pretend to be a devout Christian and a family man, but you are a fraud. Your wife can't count on you.

I was having a lot of trouble figuring out how I could make things right, to turn my life around from the downward spiral it was in.

I needed help.

I pulled into the parking lot of a little run-down office building in the Green Hills section of Nashville for an appointment with a counselor named Stephen James, who'd been recommended to me by a friend.

My guard was up, for sure. Stephen's office had a window overlooking a Ruby Tuesday and I considered: Was it too late to skip out and order potato skins?

Yes. Yes, it was.

I had some preconceived ideas about psychologists and counseling along the lines of it being something for lost, weak-minded people, involving a lot of chatting about your feelings.

Now that I was the lost one, my preconceptions were about to be challenged.

We shook hands and sat down, me eyeing him warily. Stephen has a warm demeanor, but I had always been good at stiff-arming people, keeping them at a safe distance away.

He looked me over too. He did not see a warm demeanor. He saw a disheveled man in sweatpants and a ratty T-shirt. Maybe I had brushed my hair. Probably not.

"Tell me what brings you here," he said.

"I've been going through a little bit of a tough stretch and some people thought it would be a good idea for me to talk about it," I responded.

"Do *you* think it's a good idea?"

"You are highly recommended and I have an open mind," I answered.

Stephen nodded. We both knew I hadn't answered his question. I suspect he knew I was mostly full of crap. It made me very uncomfortable. Whenever I said anything, I could tell how carefully he listened to exactly what I'd said.

That made me uncomfortable too.

Stephen asked a lot of questions: Are you willing to be completely honest with yourself and with me? Can you tell me what's going on with you right now? If we do work together, are you willing to be committed to the process, even though it will be painful at times?

I told Stephen I understood it would be painful, but of course I really didn't understand that at all. Mostly in that first meeting I bobbed and weaved and told him what I thought he wanted to hear, as if I were being interviewed on *SportsCenter*. I had spent years fine-tuning my ability to present a friendly face to the world, but letting nobody into my private, fractured piece of it. I had allowed myself to be about as vulnerable as a boulder.

Stephen saw through that immediately.

For the whole hour, I asked questions of my own, to myself. Could I trust this guy? Could I reveal to him my deepest, darkest secrets, secrets I hadn't shared with anybody else on earth?

Even as I sat in his office, I felt enormously conflicted. Part of me wanted nothing to do with therapy or delving into the past and all the pain that would come with that.

The other part was tired of hiding and telling half-truths. Did I want to keep traveling down the same grim track?

We shook hands again.

"See you next week," I told him.

All winter long, I took the creaky elevator to Stephen's third-floor office to do the work I promised I would do.

It was the hardest thing I have ever done in my life.

Finally, I worked up the courage to tell him about

the summer when I was eight. I had never told anyone about the events of that year, not even Anne.

I began: There was a teenage girl my mother hired to watch me. This girl's idea of taking care of me was to order me to take off my clothes.

She sexually abused me on numerous occasions.

The first time it happened, I thought about running away or saying no. I thought about yelling out for help.

But I didn't. She gave me orders and I followed them.

Each time it happened, I felt more wicked than the time before. By the time it stopped, I was scared and ashamed and sure I had done something terribly wrong that could only possibly be made worse if someone found out about it. No one could ever know about it. I jammed the memory of this sick teenage girl as far back in my brain as it would go and tried not to think about what would happen if a grown-up found out, or if someone confronted me about what went on.

How I wished, then and now, that was the end of it. But it wasn't. My story got worse.

Later that same year, in the waning days of September, my mother, sister, and I drove to the country to visit with family, as we often did. They lived a few hours outside of Nashville, a place with farms and barns and one-room schoolhouses, the kind of place where you didn't make play-dates, you just went out and played. I was out in the yard, throwing a tennis ball onto a roof behind a dilapidated garage. A kid who lived nearby turned up. I'd seen him before, but didn't know his name. He was maybe sixteen or seventeen years old, tall and wiry. He seemed interested in my game with the tennis ball. He walked closer and I wondered if he wanted a turn tossing the ball on the roof, seeing if he could catch it.

Oh, no. He was unzipping his pants.

I started to run, but he grabbed me. "You ain't going anywhere, kid," he said.

I struggled to get away, but it was no contest. He was rough and strong, and he forced himself on me. I closed my eyes and waited for it to be over. When people asked how I got the scratches and bruises on my face and lip, I told them I fell down in the garage.

On the ride back home, I said nothing, trying to block what happened out of my mind. But there was no forgetting. I felt filthy and bad, like I had been stained and could never be cleaned up. It was so much worse than the babysitter.

The car rolled on to Nashville, to my house. I thought of my room and my photo of Larry Bird. All I wanted was to get in my bed and pull the covers up over my head and not wake up for a long time.

I never told anyone about either of these criminals. That was a big mistake.

After these secrets were out, it was easier to talk about all the fights in school, the reckless risks I took breaking into abandoned houses, the secrets I kept from Anne, and about how certain I was that if I kept starring in sports, I could outrun my past.

I confessed the guilt and shame I've lived with, sure that if people knew the real R. A. Dickey, they would want nothing to do with him.

As the weeks turned into months, the scabs were peeled off all the old wounds. I felt raw and exposed. It was as if somebody backed up a garbage truck to my house and dumped the contents on the front lawn.

Where do I put all this stuff? How do I get rid of it?

I didn't know. But Stephen was there to help me find out how. He became the first person I ever trusted unconditionally—a skilled and steadfast guide leading me on the scariest and most important journey of my life.

Even in my pain I understood what a blessing that was.

I spent the whole winter searching for my true self and trying to feel okay with what I found. I spent it trying to reconcile with Anne and throwing my knuckleball against the gym wall and baring my soul to Stephen.

Then, a little miracle happened.

Gord Ash of the Milwaukee Brewers invited me to minor-league training camp. It was the only offer I got. Gord was the assistant general manager to Doug Melvin, who had moved on to the Brewers after the Rangers let him go.

The miraculous part was that it didn't even matter if I didn't make the big-league club. The Brewers' top farm team played in Nashville, meaning that I could continue the work with Stephen, and be close to my family.

What were the odds of that—getting my one and only offer from an organization with its top farm team in my hometown? Exactly the place I needed to be while I was fighting for my soul. I said thanks to God.

I had a ton more work to do on myself. I was learning that the truth-telling process—taking stock of who you are—isn't tidy or predictable. But as I headed off for Arizona for spring training, I felt more optimistic than I had in a long time.

I was becoming a free man.

Tell Someone

If reading my story makes you realize that you have been sexually abused, it's really important that you know three things.

You're not alone.

You can recover.

It's not your fault.

Millions of adults had similar experiences when they were kids. No matter how confused or angry or betrayed you feel about what happened, you can still have a normal life, a happy family, and a successful job. It's something that happened to you, not who you are.

Sexual abuse can make you feel like you've lost control. You may even feel responsible. You're not! Most victims are not in a position to freely say "yes" or "no." Most abuse involves someone you or your family likes or trusts, maybe even a family member, who is misusing that trust. If they're not stopped, they could hurt other kids.

If you are being or have been abused, tell an adult you trust—a teacher, counselor, school nurse, neighbor, or parent.

If they don't believe you, keep telling other adults until someone does believe you!

I can't promise talking about it will be easy. Sometimes abusers scare or threaten kids so they won't tell. But, believe me, it will be so much better for everyone involved than if you try to keep it a secret.

If you've been too confused or scared to tell anyone so far, that's okay. There's still time. Every minute is a new opportunity to get the help and support you deserve. But the longer you wait, the more damage it can cause. Act now.

You can also get help by calling 1-800-4-A-CHILD (1-800-422-4453) then push 1 to talk to a counselor. The Child Abuse Hotline is open 24 hours a day, 7 days a week. Counselors work with translators who speak 170 languages. All calls are anonymous.

Chapter 19

INTO THE MISSOURI

While I grappled with my past, my pitching performance suffered. Mightily. In my second start of the 2007 season, I got raked for eleven hits and ten runs in five innings. Next outing: seven hits and five runs, including three homers.

Start after start, I pitched glorified batting practice, doing wonderful things to opponents' batting averages. When I came out of the dugout in Nashville's Herschel Greer Stadium, or ran wind sprints in front of the big guitar-shaped scoreboard in center field, not a single soul in the crowd said, "There goes R. A. Dickey, our stopper."

I wasn't sure how close I was to being released, but if I didn't already own a home in Nashville, I wouldn't have been in the market to buy one. On June 1, my record was 3-4 and my ERA 6.24, earning me a demotion from the starting rotation.

Pitching in my hometown, in the place where I was

state prep player of the year, amplified my feeling of being a colossal failure. I reached out to Charlie Hough for help. Charlie went over all the basics we'd worked on, but he didn't have any flutterball fairy dust to sprinkle over me.

How bad was it?

Bad enough that I called a friend of a friend to ask about a job he had open in the construction supply business. My job would be to sell people insulation products. This was a phone call born of desperation. I was making $12,500 a month for the five-month minor-league season. We had a new house and a growing family. I had to formulate a backup plan in case the Brewers decided they had seen enough.

I thought about what it would be like to sell construction supplies and not to be a professional athlete anymore. I thought about having to call Charlie with the news that I'd given up the knuckleball for foam and caulk.

I couldn't do it.

But the idea that the end of my baseball career could be at hand dominated my thoughts when we traveled to the Midwest for a series against the Omaha Royals. The Sounds stayed at the same hotel I'd been at many times as a RedHawk, the Ameristar Casino Hotel in Council Bluffs, Iowa, which is just east across the Missouri River from Omaha. It is about as nice a hotel as you'll find in minor-league baseball, spacious and well-appointed and even equipped with a gift shop. Even though I dislike everything about casinos, from the recycled oxygen, to the sad soundtrack of the slots, to the desperate-looking people who don't know when to stop, I actually liked the Ameristar, mostly because it had a good bakery, with killer chocolate cake. I made the rounds on the casino floor, making sure my younger teammates were not being foolhardy with their twenty dollars in daily meal money. I always rooted for my guys to win, and not just because I'm a good teammate: When somebody hit the jackpot, it often meant an upgrade on the postgame spread, maybe barbecue and cornbread instead of the Sam's Club chicken and Van Camp's baked beans that had been on simmer since the second inning.

The elevators in the Ameristar have windows from which you get an impressive view of the Missouri River. It is big and brown, probably 250 yards across, swift of current and sludgy of texture. The first time I saw the Missouri from that elevator was in 2002 as an Oklahoma City RedHawk. Now I was a member of the

Nashville Sounds. The uniform changed, but not the fixation with the Missouri.

The absolute first thought I had when I saw the Missouri? Wouldn't it be cool to swim across that? The second thought I had was: One day I'm going to do it.

Washington crossing the Delaware, Joshua crossing the Jordan, Perseus crossing the river Styx—I thought of all these epic feats as I looked at the river. I'm no general and I'm certainly no figure from Greek mythology, but this could be my last chance to make good on the promise I had made to myself. I was only a bad outing or two away from being finished with professional baseball.

Maybe swimming across the Missouri would say something about my courage. Maybe it would prove my worth somehow—a metaphorical baptism, a renewal, a fresh start.

Maybe if I somehow got across, God would help me close the gap between the man I was and the man I wanted to be.

Or maybe I was still just a reckless fool, the way I was when I once jumped eighty feet off Foster Falls, near Sequatchie, Tennessee, or went swimming in the Atlantic Ocean during a hurricane. You could say—and some have—that I have a death wish. I think it's more accurate to say I have a risk wish, clinging to the notion that achieving these audacious feats somehow makes me special.

I'm not particularly proud that I think like this, but I admit that I do.

In the elevator, I told my roommate Chris Barnwell my plan.

"Are you out of your mind?" Chris asked. "Do you know how big that river is and how strong the currents are? That is one of the most idiotic ideas I have ever heard. Completely idiotic. You can't do this."

Chris, of course, was 100 percent right. He also figured out he wasn't getting through, so he called Anne to see if she could drive sense into me.

"He's a grown man. He knows his limitations," Anne told him. One of the things I love most about my wife is that she respects me as a man even when I act like a boy.

Word about my impending swim spread through the team like a rash. Outfielder Laynce Nix, one of my best friends on the team, emphatically joined Chris in questioning my sanity. "That's a crazy, stupid idea," he said.

Other teammates were more interested in wagering on my success, because if there's anything ballplayers love more than a spectacle, it's action. Some people picked me to make it, others didn't.

I quietly did some half-baked scouting, asking the hotel staff if it was okay to swim in the river. "Oh, God, no, you don't want to swim in the Missouri. It's dirty and the currents are strong," the half-alarmed, half-amused bellhop said.

That should have given me pause.

I plowed ahead. My idea of taking a precautionary safety measure was to buy a pair of flip-flops in the gift shop so my feet didn't get cut up on the rocky, steeply sloped banks.

Just before noon, I got into the elevator and stared at the Missouri on the ride down. I followed the course of a big log as it flowed downriver and noted how fast it was moving. Chris had given up trying to talk me out of the swim. Now he was my cornerman, pumping me up and making sure I had everything I needed.

I had the flip-flops taped to my feet. I'd studied the river and had a good plan (I actually believed this) to start upstream about a hundred yards. That way, when I got to the Nebraska side, I'd be directly opposite the hotel, ready to wave triumphantly to my adoring fans.

Small orange buoys bobbed vigorously in the middle of the river, about a hundred yards from shore. The current was much more placid near the banks. I would swim furiously to the buoys, and then throttle back for the second half, when I'd be tired. I'm a strong swimmer. I swam the two-hundred-meter freestyle when I was a kid for the Seven Hills Swim Club team.

I had no doubt I would make it across.

Fifteen or so of my teammates came to see me off. We walked through the hotel to the back. Inside the casino, it wasn't even lunchtime, but people were already busy gambling their day away. It didn't occur to me that I was about to do my own gambling. I climbed over a chain-link fence and descended the rocky bank. I stood at the river's edge—a thirty-two-year-old minor-league pitcher, husband, and father of three, in my taped-on flip-flops, and since I had neglected to pack a swimsuit for the trip to Omaha, my boxer briefs.

My teammates on the bank hooted. The guys who weren't there had their faces pressed against the hotel windows. Laynce had a video camera to record my epic feat for posterity. My own lens shifted to the water, which, up close, didn't just look brown but almost inky, with the gooeyness of motor oil.

It also looked a lot wider and faster-moving than it did from the eighth floor of the Ameristar. For an instant I wished Anne had bailed me out by seconding

Chris Barnwell's objections. Branches floated by and they were flying. The water was loud, and it was getting pretty noisy in my head too. I remembered to say a silent prayer.

I couldn't back out now. Well, I could have, but I wasn't going to. Why? Ego? Pride? Mulish stubbornness? Probably all of the above. Whatever. Something else for Stephen James and me to talk about.

I stepped into the water, up to my knees, to test the temperature. It had a cool edge to it. I didn't turn around or say anything more to my teammates. Game time. I dove in.

My adrenaline surged and I cut through the first twenty to thirty yards with powerful strokes. It was a long way to the other shore, but it wasn't going to be all that hard. Just keep wheeling those arms, I told myself.

But the farther I got out in the river, the more the current intensified. I concentrated on my cadence—one, two, three, breathe . . . one, two, three, breathe—but it was getting harder.

Sixty yards in, I had new respect for the river. I was still sure I could get across, but I changed my mind about it being easy. I dug in. Keep powering through the water and you'll get there, I told myself.

The river fought me. With each weakening stroke, it became clearer that I had greatly underestimated the power of rushing water.

As I approached the buoys and the midway point, I felt an undertow, tugging me downward. The current was stronger still. Fatigue was setting in. I picked up my head for a second, treading water, and couldn't believe where I was: a quarter mile downriver. Nebraska seemed impossibly far away. Panic swept over me.

You are in trouble, I told myself. You need to turn around.

I put my head down. I kept going.

I wasn't quitting.

I swam as hard as I ever had for the next two minutes, but this was not the Seven Hills pool. If I could get to the buoys, beyond the halfway point, I knew I could get across. But the force of the undertow was pulling at the flip-flops. I stopped to try to wrestle the things off, wasting some of my rapidly dwindling energy.

Meanwhile, the undertow made it hard to keep my head above water. I was not brave or cocksure anymore. My fantasies about a heroic crossing were as spent as I was.

Later I learned that at about this moment, Laynce

Nix put down the camcorder to pray, fearing he had seen the last of me.

I had one more push left. Which direction should I go? Forward, hoping it'll get easier once I get past the buoys? Or should I turn around and try to make it back to the bank I started from? Either way, I knew there was a very good chance I wouldn't be getting out of the Missouri River alive. A deep hopelessness swept over me.

I decided to swim back toward my teammates, who were now hundreds of yards upriver from me. I powered out fifteen strokes and had to stop, exhausted. But when I stopped, the undertow tried to pull me under. I cranked out another set of strokes, but didn't even make it to fifteen before my muscles locked up.

From out of nowhere, I thought of Michael Phelps in the Olympic pool in Athens in 2004, the way he'd push off the wall and swim underwater as long as possible before surfacing. Maybe that would work for me too.

I lasted twenty seconds before I needed air. When I submerged again, I opened my eyes and could see absolutely nothing. It was as if I was swimming in a black hole. I came back up and looked toward the Iowa bank, fifty or sixty yards away.

It might as well have been fifty to sixty miles away. I started to see gigantic spots everywhere. I was getting delirious.

I couldn't swim anymore, my stroke reduced to a pathetic dog paddle. My muscles had completely shut down. My lungs were burning and my throat felt as if I'd swallowed a thousand lit matches. Tears welled behind my eyes. I accepted that I was not going to make it out of the river. Underwater, I began to cry. It's a very odd sensation, weeping in water.

It was time to ask for forgiveness from people who would not hear me say good-bye.

Anne, I am so sorry that I am leaving you and the kids alone. I am so sorry about my stupidity and recklessness, that I'd allow an asinine attempt to prove something— I don't even know what—to take me away. I am so, so sorry.

God, please forgive all my trespasses and all the ways I've fallen short. Please give me peace.

It occurred to me that if I just opened my mouth underwater, I'd be able to apologize to God in person.

I was sinking fast now, well below the surface, when I felt solid ground beneath my very securely taped-on flip-flops.

I had hit bottom. Literally. Normally the bottom isn't

good when you are drowning, but it gave me something to push off from. I hadn't felt any spurt of adrenaline for what seemed like hours. Now, suddenly, I had one. I coiled my legs and pushed hard off the riverbed floor to power up to the surface, power up with strength I didn't think I still had.

I broke through the surface, my head out of the river. Air! I couldn't remember when I had taken my last breath. The shore was now only the distance from home to first base. How had I gotten so close? Who cares? I swam with utter fury, using my last burst of energy.

One more stroke. One more stroke, I kept telling myself.

When I lifted my head I saw Grant Balfour, a teammate, lying on his stomach on a little platform jutting out into the river. Grant is from Brisbane, Australia. He was the clubhouse barber. "Give me the Brisbane," I always told him, and he'd get out his scissors and have at it. He gives a pretty good haircut. Lucky for me, he was also good at scrambling over fences and navigating riverbanks, which was how he got to the platform.

Grant was a reliever. In the annals of baseball history, there has never been a more clearly defined save situation.

He extended his right arm, his pitching arm, as far

as it would stretch. "C'mon, R.A. You're almost there. Grab my hand," he said.

His hand was maybe eight feet away. I made a few more floundering strokes and reached out. I dog-paddled and flailed. Five feet now. I kept my eyes on Grant's hand. Grant's hand was the most important thing in my world now. Two feet away. I paddled a little more and reached, and Grant's hand clasped mine, good and strong. He hauled me toward the bank as if he were a tugboat. At the edge of the river, he wrapped his arm around me and guided me toward a small clearing, where I collapsed, sprawled on my back.

"You okay?" Grant asked.

I nodded. I stayed sprawled out for a few minutes. Eventually I clambered onto all fours. Grant helped me to my feet. I turned to look at the Missouri. I half expected to see a flying fish emerge, giving some biblical meaning to the ordeal I'd just put myself through.

The fish didn't show.

I trudged back to the hotel, Grant guiding me. When we got to the rest of the team, they checked to make sure I was still breathing before the razzing began about my oil-colored boxers, my Olympic-caliber doggy-paddling, my failed crossing. Somebody commented that if I was going to soil myself,

I should've worn a Depends. They're ballplayers. I expected nothing less.

A few of my closer friends—Chris and Laynce—quietly asked me questions and were quick to appreciate how close a call I'd just had. Back in the hotel, I threw out the boxers and took a scalding hot shower, hoping to rinse off whatever the contaminants are that had turned the river black before I sprouted a third arm.

I slept until Chris woke me up in time to get to the ballpark. I was not scheduled to pitch, of course.

As I threw in the outfield before the game that night, swells of gratitude and humility kept washing over me. I didn't have a grand epiphany in Johnny Rosenblatt Stadium on June 9, 2007. It was more subtle than that.

I dove into the water thinking I was in charge. I emerged with a powerful reminder that God was in charge. I thanked Him not just for sparing me but for teaching me. I was looking to be a hero, to use my strength to forge some sort of epic transformation. Instead, I was as humbled as a man can be, left on all fours.

God had already given me a second chance as a husband and father. He'd already given me a second chance as a pitcher. Now He had given me a second chance as a human being.

Just Say Enough

When you spend months on the road, teammates become a lot like brothers, egging each other on to keep things entertaining. The key thing about practical jokes or dares—and I learned this the hard way at the bottom of the Missouri—is to know when to stop.

Exhibit A: During spring training in 2011, Mike Pelfrey claimed he could kick a fifty-yard field goal. David Wright scoffed, betting Pelf a hundred bucks he couldn't. "This is going to be the easiest money I ever make," David said.

He was going to need to practice, so Pelf and I—40 percent of the Mets' starting rotation at the time—bought a ball and tee and headed to a football field. The gate was padlocked to keep out riffraff like us so, of course, we climbed the fence. At six feet two inches and 220 pounds, I got over without incident, but watching Pelf hoist his six-foot-seven-inch, 250-pound frame was a bit scary.

He set up at the twenty-yard line, teed up the ball, and knocked it through. Same thing at the twenty-five, the thirty, and the thirty-five. He insisted he had more yards in his leg, but by then he'd taken fifteen to sixteen hard kicks and confessed his right shin was sore.

Of course we didn't stop. Finally, Pelf teed up the ball for the fifty-yard attempt—and made it. Twice.

Then he was done. "I can't even lift my foot anymore," Pelf said. "My shin is killing me." I told him to drop the bet, and we hopped the fence again, Pelf landing with more of a thud this time. His shin hurt so much he could barely press the car's gas pedal. The last thing any of us needed was a visit to the DL because of a Stupid Human Trick.

David had a long laugh thinking about what would have happened if Pelf had gotten stuck at the top of the chain-link fence.

Chapter 20

ZEN AND THE ART OF THE KNUCKLEBALL

Three days after my swim, I went into a game in relief and pitched a scoreless inning, striking out two. A small sample, admittedly, but something felt different. Very different.

A couple of games later, I was promoted to the starting rotation again to face the Omaha Royals on a ninety-three-degree day in Nashville. I struck out the first two batters to start the game. In the third, I threw a knuckler to the Royals' first baseman, Billy Butler, and as I came through Charlie's doorframe, I felt . . . in command.

Whoa. In command was not a feeling I had felt before when throwing my knuckleball.

I wound up going seven innings, giving up just four hits and one earned run. Grant Balfour came in to get the save—a more conventional one this time—and I got the victory.

Chris Barnwell, playing second behind me, noticed something had changed too. After the game he said that while he watched me work that day, he was thinking, "The guy almost dies in the river and comes out of it a whole different person."

Okay, maybe not a whole different person, but a changed one.

I vowed not to obsess over getting back to the big leagues, or let myself feel like I was running out of time because of my age. I would not focus on the next uniform but on the next pitch, which was all I could really control.

I don't mean to make this sound like magic: Jump in a big river, cure all your problems. But here was my epiphany: As a Christian, you are supposed to seek God's will, not follow your own. You are supposed to be a believer all the time, not just when it's convenient.

I had always had a hard time surrendering control. I wanted to be in charge, to be the director of the show. I had a hard time trusting anybody, even God, to guide my life.

I had finally seen the hypocrisy in this. How could I call myself a true follower if I subconsciously believed I should be the one calling the shots?

Since Grant hauled me out of the Missouri, I decided

to trust God's plan for me. If that included a call-up to the big leagues, great. If it didn't, everything would still be okay.

Now, for the first time in my life, I was fully immersed in each moment. Maybe it's because my moments were very nearly taken away from me.

I was no longer trying to take on a river. I was flowing with it. One of the supreme paradoxes of baseball, and all sports, is that the harder you try to throw a pitch or hit a ball, the smaller your chance for success. You get the best results not when you apply superhuman effort, but when you just are—when you let the game flow organically and allow yourself to be fully present. You'll often hear scouts say of a great prospect, "The game comes slow to him." They mean that the prospect lets the game unfold in its own time, paying no attention to anything else, funneling all awareness to the athletic task at hand.

This was what was happening to me, post-Missouri. I stopped worrying about whether my knuckleball was good enough. I just threw it and reveled in the chance to do so.

Better still, I began to throw it my way. As grateful to the Rangers as I was for giving me a chance to become a knuckleballer, I never warmed to the idea of becoming a clone of Charlie or Tim Wakefield, which is what they encouraged.

"Be like Wake" didn't work. I wanted to be like me.

I'm a different pitcher than Tim Wakefield, with different strengths. Why not play to those strengths? The idea of throwing virtually every knuckler in the 60 mile an hour range just because that's what Tim did never made sense to me. I like to mix it up. Throw one at 80 miles an hour, then one at 60. Mix in an occasional fastball or cutter, just to disrupt a hitter's timing.

As the 2007 season progressed, I staked out my own knuckleballing turf. What was the worst thing that could happen? That I stayed in the minors? Maybe. But if I was serious about getting back to the big leagues, the only way it would work was to pitch my way. Once I had resistance about turning my pitching life over to the knuckleball, but that only produced uneven results. Now I planned to throw the knuckleball 80 to 85 percent of the time. And I was going to throw a lot of them fast.

After the strong start against Omaha, I was back in the rotation for the rest of the season. Five days after shutting down the Royals, I did the same to the Iowa Cubs, pitching a three-hitter into the seventh inning, and striking out eight.

I won ten out of my next eleven decisions, the best run of my entire professional career.

Chris and Grant and Laynce were there to witness my almost-drowning. They were all around too when I stopped taking on water on the mound.

"How can you explain what's going on, this change in you?" Laynce asked.

"I'm just pitching knuckleball by knuckleball, and surrendering to the results," I told him.

A Zen master of the knuckleball. That would be the territory I staked out for myself.

The last week of July, Gord Ash called. I hadn't spoken to Gord since he invited me to spring training. The Brewers were in first place and had a big four-game weekend series in St. Louis. Gord wanted to know if I'd be willing to meet the team in St. Louis and be on standby in case the club needed me to start one of the games.

"Sure, I'll be happy to meet you in St. Louis," I told him.

I'd crawl to St. Louis to meet you, I thought.

I met Gord—secretly—at the Westin Hotel in St. Louis on Friday afternoon. Because the Brewers weren't sure they'd need me, they didn't want to officially call me up and send somebody else down. Nor did they want any of the pitchers getting worked up if somebody saw me in the lobby or the restaurant, so I was under house arrest in my hotel room, complete with meal money slipped under the door. I was on lockdown each day until the club left for the ballpark. I felt like the Brewers' secret weapon, ready to be rolled into Busch Stadium when the Cardinals least expected it.

Mostly, though, I was full of hope. Hope, after all, is what kept me going.

The Brewers won big on Friday night. No call.

There was a doubleheader scheduled for Saturday, though. Obviously, they were going to need arms. I woke up early, praying to hear from Gord Ash.

No call. The Cardinals swept. Toward the end of the second game, I went for a walk, so close to Busch Stadium, I could hear the crowd and see the lights, a billion brilliant bulbs against the night sky. I hadn't been this close to a big-league park since the Massacre at Arlington, sixteen months earlier, when I surrendered the six dingers.

Was this as close as I'd ever again get to making it back? Albert Pujols or somebody must've hit a homer, because a gigantic roar went up. Being outside the ballpark, outside the action, was almost more than I could stand.

The series wrapped up Sunday, with the Cardinals winning their third in a row. My phone never rang. My weekend in St. Louis consisted of a lot of quality room service, with a side of crushed hope.

The three-hundred-mile drive back home to Nashville was long and lonely. Getting so close was testing my resolve to trust in God's plan for me.

Just keep making good starts, I told myself. That's the only thing you can control.

But would that be enough? I'd been sent back to the minors four times now. Whenever that happened, I feared disappearing forever. Out of sight, out of mind—I'd seen it happen so often. People think big-league ballplayers are at an entirely different level from Triple-A players, but the truth is that, in many cases, the difference between them is no wider than the splinter of a bat. Joe Dillon was a Sounds teammate, a corner infielder with big muscles and a healthy work ethic. He hit .317 with 20 home runs and 75 RBIs in two-thirds of a season in 2007, following up other Triple-A years in which he hit .360 with 34 homers and .329 with 39 homers and 117 RBIs.

Joe's big-league career consisted of 246 big-league at-bats with three different clubs—or about 200 more at-bats than Chris Barnwell got, even though Chris had a tremendous glove, could play anywhere, and would do all the little things it takes to win games. Chris and Joe got typecast as journeymen who were good but not good enough. The label stuck.

I had the journeyman label too, and I hated it.

I finished the year 13-6 and was voted the Pacific Coast League pitcher of the year.

The Brewers did not call me up to join the big club in September.

What more did they want me to do? How else could I prove my worth to them, beyond winning ten of my last eleven starts and being named the best pitcher in the league?

The Brewers were in a pennant race. I was their top minor-league pitcher, and they couldn't find a roster spot for me.

How could you not take that personally?

Was it my age? The knuckleball? I didn't know, but I

was sick about it. And despite my newfound commitment to serenity, I allowed myself to get angry. That was a lesson I had learned from Stephen James: Don't repress your feelings. Be honest about them. If you own the way you feel now, it won't act like poison in your system.

This was hard for me to do. I'd spent years locking sadness and anger away, toughing it out alone. I never wanted to look inside me—I was afraid of what I'd find.

But by operating that way, I buried the problem instead of dealing with it, and, inevitably, the pent-up emotions reappeared in unhealthy ways, like yelling at somebody in my family who was only trying to help.

I didn't want to be that person anymore. I sure didn't want to hurt the people whom I loved the most anymore.

And I didn't want to run away. I wanted to let people know how I felt. I wanted to be, authentically, who I was. I'd learned that when I hid or brooded or played the role of victim, the first victim was me.

The Brewers finished in second place, behind the Cardinals. As angry as I was about not getting back to the big leagues, I wasn't going to let the Brewers decide what I was capable of as a pitcher. I didn't let the lack of an ulnar collateral ligament define me. I didn't quit when I lasted exactly one start in the big leagues in 2006 before getting sent back to Oklahoma City.

Why start now?

After a short break, I got my five-gallon pail and filled it up with baseballs and threw knuckleballs by the thousands, from my meticulously manicured nails into a long white wall of cement.

I was a thirty-three-year-old free agent. God had my back. I wasn't worried about being an underdog. I love *Rocky* and *Rudy* and *The Rookie* and every overcoming-the-odds movie ever made.

Wouldn't it be nice to join that club?

Chapter 21

WHERE I WIND UP

Three hundred thousand dollars is a great salary. It's more than I'd made in the previous five years combined, and almost a quarter of a million dollars more than I made as a Nashville Sound in 2007.

I've never been one to chase the almighty dollar, but with three kids and no guarantee I'd ever see the big leagues again, how could I refuse a $300,000 offer to play in Korea for the Samsung Lions? I knew nothing about Korean baseball, other than that it was growing in popularity. I knew nothing about the Lions except that I had a Samsung DVD player once and it worked pretty well.

What I did know was that I'd just had my best minor-league season. When would my leverage ever be better?

I asked Anne about the idea of spending five months of the year in Korea. Her husband's baseball dream had already dragged her all over the place. Korea meant packing up the kids again and making the biggest transition we'd ever had to make as a family.

Anne grew up with three brothers. She is adventurous and tough.

"I'm open to it if you think it's the best career move," she said. "I'm sure the kids will adjust. It'll probably be good for them, being exposed to a different culture."

I got excited about the opportunity to make some real money. I called my agent, Bo McKinnis, who has a great gift for taking emotions out of decisions and carefully assessing the pros and cons. I told him I was leaning toward taking the Lions' offer.

There was a long silence on the other end of the line.

"I don't think that's a good idea," Bo said. "You're coming off a great year. I anticipate you having some good interest here."

"But there aren't any guarantees over here," I countered. "I was the PCL pitcher of the year and didn't even get a call-up."

"I realize that, but you have something very unique, and you are starting to figure it out," Bo said. "Korea, Taiwan, even Japan—those are places pitchers go to die. You need to realize if you go play for the Samsung Lions, the chances of you ever coming back here and playing in the big leagues are about zero."

I knew he was right: Going to Korea would likely end my dream of returning to the majors. But I was approaching my mid-thirties. Making $300K this year—and maybe another $300K the next year if I did well—was probably not going to happen in the western hemisphere. How could I refuse a possible $600K in Korea when I was a $60,000 pitcher at home?

Bo and I decided to give it a day and talk again, but the meter was running; I needed to give the Lions an answer in forty-eight hours. I was 80 percent sure I was headed for Korea. How hard, I wondered, would it be to learn to speak Korean?

A day passed and my cell phone vibrated. I could tell from the number it was Bo. I considered saying hello in Korean (*An-nyeong-ha-se-yo*), but Bo might not have appreciated my joke.

"I've got some news for you," he said. "The Minnesota Twins, the Seattle Mariners, and the New York Mets are all interested in you. I don't have the particulars of their offers yet, but I will soon."

"That's good news—very good, but I have to give the Korean team my answer today," I told him. This was not what Bo wanted to hear.

"R.A., please trust me on this," he said. "There is real interest in you. Korea will be there whenever you want, but if you take it now, you will regret it. You are this close to busting through. I'd hate to see you do something that you'll regret."

Decision time was at hand. I didn't want to string the Lions along.

The word "regret" echoed in my mind. Voice One and Voice Two returned:

VOICE ONE: What's to decide? You have one guarantee and it's in Korea. It's the only assurance you have that you'll make at least a year or two years' worth of decent money.

VOICE TWO: Aim high. You can take guaranteed money now, but how much money is that guarantee going to cost you down the line?

VOICE ONE: You are thirty-three years old and haven't pitched in the big leagues in two years. What Kool-Aid are you drinking, thinking teams are going to line up to hand you a big-league uniform?

VOICE TWO: You are getting better at your craft. Knuckleballers can pitch forever.

VOICE ONE: Be prudent.

VOICE TWO: Be brave.

The voices had at it, until finally Voice Two shouted down Voice One.

Sure, Korea was safe, locked-up money. But choosing Korea was choosing to settle. I would never find out how good I could be as a knuckleballer—never find out if I could, indeed, make it back from the six-home-run game.

I called the Samsung Lions' representative and told him thanks, but no thanks.

I called Bo and told him: Get me a deal. I knew he was smiling on the other end of the line.

Bo talked to the Mets, the Mariners, and the Twins, trying to find the best spot. The Twins were the most stable organization of the three, and seemingly the best shot to make it back to the big leagues. So right after Thanksgiving 2007, I signed a minor-league deal that included an invitation to the Twins' spring training camp in Fort Myers, Florida, and a chance to make the big club.

It felt sweet to be wanted.

Days later, the baseball winter meetings began at the Opryland hotel in Nashville, an irresistibly short commute from my house. I ventured over to meet Bill Smith, the Twins' general manager, along with manager Ron Gardenhire. Granddaddy always told me it's a good idea to look your bosses in the eye to show them that you respect them, but that you aren't scared of them.

I got on the elevator, and caught myself scripting something in my head to make a good first impression. *Stop it. Just be yourself.*

I shook hands with Smith and Gardenhire but immediately sensed I'd walked into a tense situation. Twins management was smack in the middle of deciding whether to trade their longtime ace, Johan Santana, to the Mets in exchange for a package of young players. It was time to act and there was a vigorous debate going on as to whether they should make the deal.

"Go ahead and trade him," I said. "I can pick up his slack." Everybody laughed, taking my idle boast in the right spirit. I kind of surprised myself with that comment, but I guess I was just being myself. I got out of there before I could be any more of myself.

The next day I got a phone call from a reporter. "Hey, R.A., how does it feel to be the newest member of the Seattle Mariners?"

"You mean the Twins?" I responded. "It feels great. I feel like they will give me—"

He stopped me. "No, it's the Mariners. You didn't

hear? They just took you in the Rule 5 draft."

I was at a loss for words. A Mariner? I thought the Twins wanted me. That was quick. Did my Santana comment come back to bite me?

I told the reporter I'd call him back, and minutes later the Mariners called. It was true. The Rule 5 draft is a Major League Baseball provision aimed at preventing teams from stockpiling players in the minors when other clubs would be willing to give them a chance to play in the majors. Since I was not yet on the Twins' forty-man roster, I was eligible to be plucked—and that's what the Mariners did, paying $50,000 for me.

On one hand, it was a good sign that they liked me enough to steal me from the Twins, but it was still a completely bewildering development. I had already imagined myself in a Twins uniform, moving Anne and the kids to Minneapolis. Now this. Could there possibly be any more plot twists in my baseball life?

I showed up for spring training at the Mariners' camp in Peoria, Arizona, and pitched as both a starter and a reliever. I had one of the best springs of my life. I knew my knuckleball was dancing because Kenji Johjima, the Mariners catcher, caught only about three out of every ten I threw. The other seven hit him in the shin guards or the mask, or he had to chase them back to the screen. I encouraged him to switch to the oversized glove that virtually all catchers use to catch the knuckleball, but he was very attached to his regular Mizuno.

I was one of the leaders of the Cactus League in innings pitched and ERA that spring, with one more appearance before opening day, against the Giants. It was my strongest outing yet, getting the win by giving up only one hit over six innings. I left the game as elated as I'd been in a long time. It'd been two years since the six-homer game, and I thought I could now finally start my big-league career anew, in the great Northwest, pitching not to survive but to flourish, to be a craftsman with my knuckleball. I felt so grateful to Bo McKinnis for talking me out of Korea.

Our last exhibition game was in Las Vegas against the Cubs. I found myself wondering what the Mariners' clubhouse looked like and how nice it would be to have a locker there. When the game ended, I packed my bag and gave it to the clubhouse attendant. I put on a suit and walked toward the plane that would take the team to Seattle, when I saw Lee Pelekoudas, the assistant general manager, waving to flag me down.

He must be coming to congratulate me, I thought.

"R.A., I'm sorry to have to tell you this, but you didn't make the team," Lee said.

My mouth literally dropped open. I honestly thought: This must be a joke. Let's pull a prank on the new guy and see how amusing his reaction is.

I was not amused. Lee could see I was not amused.

"I know you're disappointed, but I want you to know we like you a lot, so we made a trade to keep you," he said.

Under Rule 5 regulations, clubs that lose a player can get that player back for $25,000 if the club that selected him doesn't put him on the big-league roster. The Twins bought me back, and then the Mariners traded a minor-league catcher, Jair Hernandez, in order to keep me.

"We are keeping you on the forty-man roster," Lee continued. "You just didn't make the opening-day roster."

Jaw still dropped. Lee walked away.

Moments passed in silence as my anger built. Why did I keep getting passed over? I pitched my butt off all last year and the Brewers never called me up. Then I pitched my butt off all spring, ended it with a six-inning one-hitter, and was told I was not good enough. Was this more of the baseball-people-don't-trust-the-knuckleball crap?

What on earth did I have to do? I wanted to let God have it, when general manager Bill Bavasi came over. I let him have it instead.

"You're mad, aren't you?" he said.

"You bet I'm mad."

"You have a right to be mad. You pitched great. I'd be mad too. Just don't stay mad, because we are going to need you," he said.

Slowly, I calmed down. I appreciated Bill's words, and though I remained confounded by the club's decision, I didn't think he was feeding me a line of bull.

I called Anne to break the bad news, and she insisted on coming to Seattle anyway. We drove around Tacoma, home of the Mariners' Triple-A affiliate, the Rainiers, and found a little rental house up the hill from Puget Sound. It was a sweet place in an idyllic setting. A consolation prize, yes, but a nice one.

Apart from not being in the big leagues, Tacoma is a great place to pitch. The air is cool, the grass long, the fences tall. I lost my first couple of decisions, but I pitched deep into the games. We just didn't score any runs. I hated losing, but my knuckleball was not to blame.

The hitters' swings will tell you if your knuckleball

is any good. That's the only feedback you need, Charlie always says. I was getting a lot of ugly swings, and wild misses.

True to Bavasi's word, the Mariners called me up in mid-April. I drove to Seattle as if the invitation had an expiration date. I was deliriously happy but privately paranoid. What if this was another one of those deals like the time the Brewers asked me to join them in St. Louis, then sent me right back down?

Walking up to Safeco Field felt surreal. I always wanted to believe I'd get back to the big leagues, but a small demon voice inside me continually whispered that I was done, used up, that I could not recover from the six-homer game, or my deeper past.

I had listened to that voice for too many years. I was done paying attention.

Get lost, I told the demon.

After I got my uniform (number 41) and said hello to my new teammates, including Ichiro, Raul Ibañez, and Adrian Beltre, I shook hands with the manager, John McLaren, and the pitching coach, Mel Stottlemyre, who sent me to the bullpen—for now.

I spent my first big-league practice in two years shagging flies in right field, in my new favorite American

League park, which is friendly to pitchers and stunning to look at, with a giant retractable roof, and steel and iron latticework, and grass so vivid it should have its own name: Safeco green. I savored every minute.

We were playing the Kansas City Royals, our starter Jarrod Washburn going against Zack Greinke. At Safeco, a dark blue cinder-block wall separates the home bullpen from the visiting bullpen. Each inning I threw ten balls against the wall, monitoring the spin and feeling my release point. It was like I was back in Uncle Ricky's gym.

The game moved quickly. Greinke cruised and Jarrod gave up three runs through six. The Royals extended the lead to 5–1 in the top of the eighth. When the phone rang in the bullpen, it was the dugout calling to deliver the message: R.A.'s got the ninth.

Greinke threw another scoreless inning, and then I was up. I felt more excited than nervous, fearless in Seattle. My leg did not quiver; my heart did not race. I thanked God not just for this opportunity but for the blessing to live in the moment fully.

David DeJesus, a speedy guy with some pop in his bat, was up first. I fell behind 2-0, but worked him to a 3-2 count. He popped out on a fastball. I threw a lively knuckleball to get ahead on Mark Grudzielanek, the Royals' number two hitter, before getting him to ground out with a fastball on the outside of the plate.

The third hitter, Mark Teahen, was one of their power guys. I like facing guys who have power, because they swing hard. A hard swing and a good knuckleball is the combination a knuckleball pitcher dreams of. I went up 0-2 on a couple of good knuckleballs and, on 1-2, threw a wicked knuckler that seemed to have its own gravitational pull, stopping midair, twice, before it started toward the plate again. It was one of the best knuckleballs of my life.

Teahen missed it by about a foot.

I walked off the field feeling as light and happy as you can feel when you are down four in the ninth. My one-inning reentry to the major leagues couldn't have gone any better. In the clubhouse afterward, a few writers asked me about how it felt to be back. I told the truth about how emotional it was. I fought back tears, and that was okay.

Forty-five minutes later, after a nice dinner in the clubhouse, I walked down the tunnel to the dugout to sit on the bench and take in the quiet afterglow of an empty stadium. The grounds crew was raking around the bases.

In the two years since my previous big-league appearance, I'd almost lost my marriage, nearly drowned in the Missouri, and finally let go of my terrible secret. In the warm light of Safeco Field, I thanked God for the gift of being there, then paused to take in a few things—the splendor of a ballpark that looked like Oz, the peace growing inside me, and a feeling that the best was yet to come.

Chapter 22

THE JEDI COUNCIL OF KNUCKLEBALLERS

Part Two: Wake

The world champion Red Sox came to Seattle at the end of May, and for me that didn't mean Manny and Ortiz or Dustin Pedroia. It meant Tim Wakefield, the only full-time knuckleballer in the game besides me. I got to the park early on Memorial Day afternoon and had the clubhouse guy deliver a note to Tim, asking if we could meet.

Meet me behind the plate in ten minutes, Tim answered.

We talked for forty-five minutes. Tim is a warm and generous man, one of the nicest people in the game, and I took full advantage, firing questions at him the way I did with Charlie and with Coach Forehand in my "Lapdog" days. I wanted to know about his grip, his nails, his tricks for killing spin. I wanted to know it all.

"Do you ever worry that one day you'll get out there and you just won't have it? About the pitch just deserting you?" I asked.

"That never happens," he said.

I envied his confidence. I still felt insecure about my knuckleball, anxious that one day it would abandon me, flit away like a hummingbird, never to return.

Tim was throwing a bullpen session that day, so I asked if I could watch. He checked with the Sox pitching coach, who said sure. Here's the knucklehead brotherhood in play again: There's no chance that an opposing pitcher, no matter how nice a guy, is going to invite me to watch how he grips and throws his split-fingered fastball or his slider. Those are state secrets.

Knuckleballers don't keep secrets. It's as if we have a greater mission beyond our own fortunes. And that mission is to pass it on, to keep the pitch alive. Maybe that's because we are so different, and the pitch is so different, but I think it has more to do with the fact that this is a pitch that almost all of us turn to in desperation. It is what enables us to keep pitching, stay in the big leagues, when everything else has failed. So we feel gratitude toward the pitch. It becomes way more than just a means to get an out.

It becomes a way of life.

Tim threw forty pitches in his bullpen. I studied everything he did. His consistency was tremendous, and for me that was the biggest difference between us. My best knuckleball was on par with his best knuckleball, but his so-so knuckleball was much better than my so-so knuckleball. He threw seven to eight out of ten knuckleballs that were really good. I was more in the six to seven range.

But what I learned from Tim was that not every one has to be perfect. I drove myself batty trying to make every one perfect.

"They just have to be good enough to get an out," Tim said. He emphasized the importance of arm path: bringing your arm through in the same way, down the center of your body, as if you were going to knock your pitching hand into your cup.

I thanked Tim profusely when he finished, and went to my own bullpen, throwing my own knuckleball, trying to get better. Tim inspired me again two days later when he shut us down over eight innings, giving up five hits and a single run, striking out eight and walking nobody.

It was a masterful performance, but Erik Bedard, Brandon Morrow, and J. J. Putz were a little better, combining for a two-hit shutout. I could never root against my own team, even with Tim pitching, but I got the next best thing: a knuckleballer pitching brilliantly and dominating big-league hitters, and my team winning the game.

I had my best stretch of pitching as a knuckleballer over the next six weeks. I was getting ahead in counts, changing speeds, throwing with conviction, and when I put together a fourteen-inning scoreless streak out of the pen, I started to think I was narrowing the gap between Tim and me. We flew to Toronto to take on the Blue Jays and I went into a game in the bottom of the eighth with the score tied 2–2. I struck out pinch hitter Brad Wilkerson to get started, then got Lyle Overbay and Marco Scutaro on groundouts.

In the bottom of the ninth, Scott Rolen came up with the winning run at third. I got him to bounce out to force extra innings, and we won in ten on Miguel Cairo's suicide squeeze.

Putz came in and got the save.

I got my win; my first big-league victory in almost three years.

Chapter 23

THE JEDI COUNCIL OF KNUCKLEBALLERS

Part Three: An Appointment with Dr. Phil

Three doors down from my locker in the Mariners clubhouse was the baseball home of Ichiro Suzuki, a hit-making marvel. I'd spent my whole career seeking consistency, so I was keen to observe the ways of Ichiro, a wiry little man who had won ten straight Gold Gloves, and had more than 200 hits in each of his first ten years in the majors.

Ichiro's act, however, would be tough to replicate. His preparation was calibrated to the minute; from the time he arrived each day to when he used the bathroom before the game. He took the same number of swings in the cage during batting practice. He ate the same pregame meal (a salmon rice ball) at the same time (ninety minutes before game time). His stretching routine was so thorough and intricate, he could have moonlighted as a contortionist for Cirque du Soleil. He is a perfectionist in every way. Though he speaks English quite well, he insisted interviews be conducted in Japanese, with an interpreter at his side, because he worried he might get a word wrong.

His approach over 162 games never varied. Nothing changed regardless of the results. The man is so vigorously regimented that you have to simply surrender to the fact that you could try to match his discipline, but you never will.

But Ichiro inspired me with his preparation, motivating me to ramp up my own readiness. The key to good knuckleballing is having the same feel for the pitch, over and over. That means having the same grip on the ball, the same release, the same follow-through. If anything is off even slightly, the ball is going to rotate and your outings are going to be brief.

Working out of the bullpen, I felt I'd finally found my niche at the big-league level. I'd given up just three runs in my last twenty innings and walked only five, while striking out thirteen.

Flying back to Seattle from Toronto, Mel Stottlemyre, our pitching coach, wandered to the back of the plane and sat down next to me. "R.A., you've been throwing the ball well, and we want to start you next week against the Nationals," he said.

I gulped but tried to disguise it. "Whatever the club needs is fine with me," I said.

Mel returned to the front. I felt a stab of guilt, because I just lied to Mel, another pitching coach who is one of the all-time good guys. The truth was, I didn't

R.A.'S TIPS FOR YOUNG PITCHERS

Learn to love stretching. *Increasing your flexibility not only helps prevent injury, but it can also add velocity to your fastball by giving you a fuller range of motion. Stretch different parts of your body—legs, back, shoulders, neck. Pitching involves your whole body, not just your arm.*

want to go into the Mariners' rotation. I knew it was a compliment to be asked to take on a bigger role, but my entire career had been a high-wire act in which I'd fallen into the net too many times to count. I was finally in a place, in the pen, where I could pitch effectively. I didn't want to mess with it.

But I didn't feel like I could say that to Mel or anybody else.

I wanted to have faith in myself, but my career felt about as sturdy as a house of toothpicks. Move one and the whole thing might crumble.

So I took the start against the Nationals in Seattle. I gave up a run in the first, and six in the second, the Nationals lighting me up like a Roman candle. I lasted for just an inning and a third.

My second start was another award winner. This time the ruination of my ERA came courtesy of the Florida Marlins, who scored five runs off me in three and two-thirds innings. For those of you keeping score at home, that's twelve runs in five and a third innings as a starter.

My momentum was trashed and I had no one to blame but myself. I pitched without conviction that I could throw my knuckleball for strikes, so the minute I fell behind a batter I threw 85 mile per hour fastballs. I pitched afraid, like I did in the six-home-run game against the Tigers, throwing it up there and hoping for the best. I thought I was beyond that. Apparently I wasn't.

I tried to channel my inner Ichiro, but my knuckleball was all over the place. Some days I emphatically trusted the pitch and did great; other times I abandoned it at the first sign of trouble, terrified to make a mistake.

I finished the year in the pen, pitching just well enough to not get sent down. For the season, my ERA in the pen was under 3.0, but as a starter it was 6.72. In November, the Mariners released me, which meant for the third time in my career, I was a free agent.

Despite my ups and downs, I thought I'd shown enough in my good moments that somebody might want me, and the somebody turned out to be the Twins again. They signed me to a contract and offered an invitation to spring training.

Before camp, I decided I needed to see another therapist. Not for my head, but for my pitch, and who better to consult than a specialist—Hall of Famer Phil Niekro.

I called Phil and introduced myself.

"I know who you are," he said. "I've seen you on TV a couple of times this year."

We met the following week in Atlanta, at an indoor baseball facility near his home.

"Let's get to work," he said. I popped a DVD into my laptop, a video of one of the stronger games I had over the year.

"I want to see one of your bad games," Phil said. "We learn more from those."

Phil watched the bad game intently. But two line-drive base hits into my outing, he told me to stop the machine.

"Watch your hips, R.A.," he said. "You're losing so much finish by not firing your hips toward the plate, not getting your backside involved."

I saw instantly what he meant. My right foot stayed behind, as if glued to the rubber, robbing me of explosion toward the plate, and the hand speed that comes with it. Obviously, the knuckleball isn't a power pitch, so the point isn't to generate speed for the sake of speed. The point is that by firing the hips forward, bringing the body toward the plate in a single, tight motion, you keep your body properly aligned and greatly increase your chances of killing rotation and throwing a good, hard knuckleball with sharp, late movement—or finish, as we like to say.

"Your knuckleball is lazy," Phil said. "You need to give it energy."

We moved to a mound and I started throwing, trying to implement Phil's suggestions. I focused on my hips and detaching my right foot from the rubber.

With every throw, I felt myself almost hop toward the plate, a sign that I was getting my hips involved. I saw results immediately. One after another, knuckleballs came out with no spin, dropping by the foot.

I felt like I could throw for hours. Before I even got off the mound, I was full of gratitude, not just for Phil, but also for Charlie and Tim—for their expertise and their generosity of spirit. All three of them opened themselves up to help a knuckleballer in need. I was part of a brotherhood; the only prerequisite for admission, a passion for the pitch.

"This has just been a tremendous help," I told Phil as I packed up my stuff. I had five hundred dollars in my pocket. I wanted to pay him something for his time, and his expertise. He refused to take it.

"My pleasure, R.A.," he said. "You're a good athlete, I can see that. Remember to be one on the mound as well. If you keep working on being an athlete and getting your hips involved, I think you're going to get where you want to go."

I drove north out of Atlanta on Interstate 75, feeling like I'd just been given the last big piece of a complicated puzzle. Thanks to Charlie, I had the proper grip and the awareness of coming through the doorframe. Thanks to Tim Wakefield, I had the right arm path, releasing the ball and bringing my arm through toward my cup. Thanks to Phil, I was firing my hips and exploding toward the plate, an action that was giving my ball a devastating finish before it got to the plate.

"You have an angry knuckleball," Phil told me. "It comes in so much harder than the way guys have historically thrown the pitch. That's a tremendous asset if you can harness it."

I spent the remaining days before spring training refining my delivery, making sure the puzzle pieces fit snugly together. The difference in the quality of my knuckleball was staggering. I used to throw maybe three out of ten that had a big late break; now it was happening with almost every one I threw properly. The only downside was nobody wanted to catch me. A few college kids took turns, but I started to notice that when I showed up with a glove and a bucket of balls, they suddenly remembered pressing commitments.

In my first official minute as a member of the Minnesota Twins, I slipped into an old habit. I walked into the clubhouse of their spring training complex in Fort Myers, Florida, and looked for my locker and number. Not so I could put my stuff down; so I would know, immediately, what my standing with this club was.

If your locker is in the same neighborhood as the team stars—Joe Mauer or Justin Morneau, for instance—and your jersey has a number in the thirties or forties, that is the best possible news. If your locker adjoins the bullpen catcher's and there's a number 81 shirt hanging in it, you're probably not going to make the forty-man roster.

My space was in a row with Joe Nathan and Francisco Liriano; my number, 39. These were signs the Twins had confidence in me, and I did my best to fulfill their—and my—hope. In outing after outing, I filled the strike zone with as fierce a knuckleball as I have ever had. Facing the Orioles in Sarasota, I threw three knuckleballs to Brian Roberts, their second baseman, and he missed all three, the last one so badly that the bat flew into the stands and Roberts' response was to giggle. When knuckleballers get the giggle response—which means the batter is completely flummoxed and utterly embarrassed—you know you're having a good day.

I worked both as a starter and a reliever, with equally good results. I finished the spring with eighteen strike-outs in seventeen innings, four walks, and a 2.02 ERA.

Camp was almost over when Gardy summoned me to his office. Gardy is Ron Gardenhire, the manager.

I didn't want to think about 2008, when I pitched my tail off for the Mariners and got sent to Tacoma. I wanted to hope for the best, but given my history of failure and disappointment, you can understand why I didn't.

"Have a seat," Gardy said. "We all love the way you've thrown the ball this spring," he told me. "You've been solid or better than that in every appearance."

I was bracing for the "but." But it never came.

"You're on the team, R.A.," Gardy said. "Scott Baker is going to start the season on the DL, and we want you to start the fifth game against the White Sox."

Thank you, Gardy. I did not jump up and down even though I wanted to.

It would be my fourth time on an opening-day roster, but my first since 2006. I felt euphoric, but I also felt dizzy from the unending ebb and flow of my career: I'm up. I'm down. Up. Down. Up and down again. Now I was up again, and I said a prayer to thank God for giving me the strength to persevere.

Dear God, I am so grateful for the chance to live in the present unhindered by a past that had once haunted me. I am scared, but I am excited about my start on Friday.

I wanted to ask God to give me whatever I needed to stay in the big leagues for a while, to allow me to have the one thing I had never had: a sustained run of success, a chance to be a truly valued member of a big-league pitching staff.

I didn't pray for this. I didn't want to be greedy.

Despite the weather, my first start went well in Chicago. It was thirty-nine degrees at game time, with wind gusts of twenty-five miles per hour. It felt like pitching in the Arctic Circle, but I got through five innings and got the victory over José Contreras. The best part was having Anne and our daughters in the stands (Eli was still too young to spend a night in the Arctic Circle). Gabriel and Lila were so filled with love and pride for their dad that it fueled my determination to be a father worthy of their love. When I started working with Stephen James, he told me something I've never forgotten.

If you aren't willing to work through whatever problems you have, you might as well wrap them up with a bow and give them to your children. Because they will inherit whatever your issues are, unless you are willing to do the work to get rid of them.

So I did the work, every day, and I began to see big payoffs. Seeing my children happy was the greatest motivator of all. Too often in the past I would be short with them, particularly before I had a start. They deserved better. The work I was doing was helping me see that, and be a better father.

Scott Baker returned from the DL and I went to the pen, which was the plan all along. My knuckleball was not quite as sharp as it was in the spring, but it was still coming out of my hand well. The Royals came to town to play a weekend series in early May. The big news for the Twins was that our All-Star catcher, Joe Mauer, was coming off the disabled list, ready to start the season.

The Saturday game was a wild affair, 7–7 in the top of the eleventh. Craig Breslow walked the bases loaded and Gardy called for me out of the pen. A tough spot, made tougher because Joe had never caught me before. Honestly, I wasn't sure if he had ever caught a knuckleball.

Gardy handed me the ball. "Don't throw your knuckler in this situation," he said. "Work with your fastball and slider. We don't want Joe chasing it to the backstop and runners scoring, okay?"

I was dumbfounded. Don't throw my knuckler? That was how I got people out. Throw my slider? Um, I didn't even throw a slider. I looked at Joe. He shrugged and ran back behind the plate. This turn of events unsettled me. I should have been able to shake it off at this stage of my career, but I let it get into my head. I went up 1-2 on the Royals' designated hitter, John Buck, but I was trying to do too much, feeling acute pressure to put my fastball in precise spots.

On the eighth pitch of the at-bat—all fastballs—I walked Buck, forcing in the go-ahead run. I wanted to scream. The one thing I couldn't do in that situation, walk the guy, I did. The Royals had the lead now without even getting a hit.

I got the next hitter, Alberto Collaspo, to ground out on a sinker, but David DeJesus singled in a run on another fastball. I'd had enough. I called Joe out to the mound.

"Listen, Joe, I know you haven't caught me before, but I've got to throw my knuckleball. That's the reason I'm here," I told him.

"Let it rip," Joe said. "I'll be fine."

I hit Miguel Olivo with a knuckleball, and then got Tony Peña to ground out to end the inning. I didn't get the loss, and didn't even get the runs charged to me, since Breslow had put them on, but I felt responsible for the loss. I was decompressing, unhappily, at my locker when Gardy came by.

"I'm sorry I put you in that position," he said. "I should've known better."

"Don't worry about it," I told him. "It happens. I appreciate your apology."

I headed to the shower, impressed that Gardy would own up to a bad decision. It's a glimpse into why he's such a good manager of people and why his players like him so much. Gardy may have messed up in that case, but he took responsibility for it. The ability to say the words "I'm sorry" is one of the greatest healing agents in the world. I wonder how many managers would be secure enough to do such a thing.

My guess is: Not many.

I recovered from my Royals outing and pitched well for the rest of the first half. In ten appearances in June, I gave up only eight hits and one run, lowering my ERA to 2.36. It was the most sustained success I'd had as a knuckleballer. I'd synthesized all I'd learned from Charlie, Phil, and Tim, and added my own personality to the pitch as well. I was also getting a lot of work, so that throwing it was becoming instinctual, with a repeatable delivery, which made for a much higher percentage of strikes.

I played catch virtually every day with either Kevin Slowey, my best friend on the team, or Nate Dammann, the bullpen catcher. They wound up chasing a lot of balls, instead of catching them, a sign that my knuckleball was doing what it was supposed to.

After the All-Star break, Kevin developed a wrist injury and couldn't be a catch partner anymore. Nate got other duties assigned to him, so in the span of days I lost both my catchers. The only guy left without a partner was Joe Nathan, our star closer, whose catch partner had just been claimed off waivers.

Joe and I were friends, so we partnered up after the break. The only problem was *it was Joe Nathan*. I didn't want our All-Star closer to take a knuckleball on the knee or have to chase the thing into the far-flung crevasses of the Metrodome. So I started backing off my repetitions. I worried more about Joe's work than my own. I made sure he got his work in, but I reduced the number of knuckleballs I threw by half during our pre-batting-practice catch time. Gradually I started to lose my feel. I needed repetitions and wasn't getting them. It wasn't Joe's fault, it was mine, for not finding a way to do the work, no matter what.

Faster than you can say "designated for assignment," I regressed into the R.A. of a year or two before. After the break, I got knocked around so badly, my ERA jumped to the fours, the low point coming in Anaheim against the Angels, who pummeled me for four hits and three runs in a third of an inning.

In early August, the Twins acquired Carl Pavano and needed a spot on the roster.

Guess who was selected to provide it?

Back to Triple-A I went, the newest member of the Rochester Red Wings, one of the few minor-league teams I hadn't played for, or so it felt. I went into the rotation and I got spanked around. I did not get a September call-up. It was my own doing, I know that, but it felt as though the knuckleball naysayers—a club with a very sizable membership—were much quicker to bury a knuckleballer than a conventional pitcher.

Was I making excuses? Deluding myself?

R.A.'S TIPS FOR YOUNG CATCHERS

How to Catch a Knuckleball

Catching a knuckleball is one of the hardest and most thankless tasks in baseball. There's a famous quote from Bob Uecker, who spent part of his major-league career catching Phil Niekro, that the only way to do it is to "wait until it stops rolling and then pick it up."

My catcher Josh Thole made huge strides during our years as battery mates on the Mets. Here's what it's like to catch me, in Josh's own words:

Catching a knuckleball is a mentally draining assignment, because you have to concentrate so hard and be so alert just to get the thing in your glove. I use a Rawlings Spark that belongs to R.A. It's a women's softball catcher's glove, and about one-third bigger than a regular catcher's glove. If I still used a regular glove, I'd be going to the backstop every pitch.

R.A.'s knuckleball can break so much and so late, it's almost like you have to surround the pitch rather than catch it.

I used to give R.A. a target, the way I do with conventional pitchers.

I was so much more self-aware than I'd ever been before, but did I have a great big blind spot, as big as the mound itself? Was I in denial?

No, I didn't think I was in denial. In my heart and soul, I believed I was getting progressively better as a knuckleball pitcher. I sincerely thought I could be a

But when you do that, you have a tendency to have a stiff wrist and to reach out for pitches, which you can't do with the knuckleball. Doug Mirabelli, who caught Tim Wakefield for years, advised me to keep the glove relaxed, resting on my left knee, so now I don't hold the glove up at all; it's down, like I'm not even expecting a pitch. That simple change has made all the difference because it makes it easier to track the flight of the ball.

The other change Doug suggested was to angle my body toward the second baseman. That clears my knees out of the way and leaves my glove hand closer to the plate, ready to snag the pitch after it breaks.

Doug also reassured me that no matter how good a catcher you are, if you're the primary person catching the knuckleballer on your staff, you're going to lead the league in passed balls. There's no way around it. Hearing that helped me relax. The pitch is hard enough to catch without getting down on yourself about errors.

contributing member of a big-league pitching staff. If you wanted to look at my history and argue otherwise, okay. But I knew my pitch, and myself, and I knew both of us were on the upswing.

I just needed one more chance.

Would any team give me a chance?

My agent's phone rang.

The caller was Omar Minaya, general manager of the New York Mets.

Chapter 24

A BITE OF THE BIG APPLE

The Dickey Baseball Tour Across America arrived in Buffalo, New York, in April 2010. Stops had included the Dust Belt (Oklahoma City), the Coffee Belt (Seattle), and the Shuffleboard Belt (Port Charlotte, Florida), so it's only fitting that, finally, I hit the Snow Belt.

I rented a two-bedroom apartment over a garage, and purchased bedding at Wal-Mart —three inflatable mattresses: a double for Anne and me, another double for our girls, Gabriel and Lila, and a single raft for Eli.

I wanted to believe there was good reason for making my family sleep on inflatable mattresses in the Snow Belt, but my new team—the New York Mets—was not making it easy. I signed with the Mets mostly because I knew Omar Minaya from our days in Texas and I felt his interest was sincere. He'd tried to sign me for the past two years, so that had to mean something, right?

Omar told me the same fib every team tells free-agent pitchers—"You're going to have a chance to make the rotation"—but when I got to camp, I saw squadrons of pitchers, all trying to make the team. Well, it seemed like squadrons of them; maybe two dozen. It's hard to have confidence when you've bounced around as many Belts as I have. A month into camp, Dan Warthen, the pitching coach, stopped by my locker to tell me the manager wanted to see me in his office. The Mets' manager was Jerry Manuel, the same guy who basically called me the twelfth-best pitcher on a twelve-man staff when I came on in relief against his White Sox in 2001.

It was March 15, 2010. There were still two weeks left of the exhibition season. Jerry, apparently, had seen enough. "We're sending you out to the minor-league side," he said. "Go down there and get your work in. We know you will be a professional."

I was the first player cut that spring. Not the second, or the third. The first.

When I reported to the minor-league complex, Terry Collins, who ran that department at the time, had more bad news: Minor-league players were not allowed to have beards.

I'd had my beard for six years. I'd grown fond of it. There was no way in which it interfered with my pitching. I asked about an exemption for a thirty-five-year-old man with a wife and three kids. The answer was no.

So the kids and I gathered on the porch of our rental house and made a family project out of shaving Daddy's beard. Everybody got a turn with the clippers. As I rubbed my bare chin for the first time since 2004, I wondered again where the heck I was going with this increasingly far-fetched dream. Perseverance is usually a virtue, but there's a time when you have to stop messing around with your grip and be a grown-up.

In the morning, I called Lipscomb University in Nashville to talk to an admissions officer. I told her I had attended the University of Tennessee but had left school a year short of getting my degree in English literature. I asked if there was a way I could transfer my credits to Lipscomb so I could finish my education. She thought there probably was and asked me to have UT send her a copy of my college transcript so she could see where I stood.

My new idea was to look for a job teaching English, but obviously I needed a college degree first. I remembered what a positive impact Miss Brewer at MBA had on me. It was exciting to imagine myself in a high school classroom, teaching English. With a beard.

What would it be like to be a college student again, fourteen years after I'd left school to pursue professional baseball? Would I be happier reading Tolstoy than trying to throw a knuckleball by Tulowitzki? Maybe.

School wouldn't start until the fall, however, so the mound remained my office for the moment. And maybe if I did well in Buffalo, I'd get a shot at working at company headquarters in New York City.

But would I really get a fair shot, even if I performed spectacularly? From what I'd heard, Omar and Jerry needed the club to start strong just to hold on to their jobs. Would they entrust their futures to a geriatric knuckleballer who had a total of twenty-two career victories and seemed to have been knocking around baseball since dinosaurs walked the earth?

My first start as a Buffalo Bison was against the Scranton/Wilkes-Barre Yankees, and I got roughed up a bit, giving up six runs in five innings. I recovered by pitching into the seventh inning and beyond in my next two starts.

My last start in April had me facing the Durham Bulls, the best-hitting team in the International

League. It was also a home game on a brutally cold night, the wind whipping furiously off of Lake Erie. Fans of the Herd (as the Bison are lovingly called) are hardy stock, but even they knew better than to come out for April baseball on that night. There were about 300 people in the stands.

Fernando Perez, a switch-hitting outfielder, led off for Durham. I went up on him 0-2 before floating a knuckleball toward the plate. He got under it and popped it weakly over second base, where it plopped in for a single.

I retired the next twenty-seven hitters in order.

Let me write that sentence one more time: I retired the next twenty-seven hitters in order. I think that is the most fun sentence I will ever write.

A perfect game, with one mulligan.

I'd never had another game quite like it—not many people have! Whoever heard of twenty-eight up, twenty-seven down?

I threw only three or four fastballs out of ninety pitches. The knuckleballs had some crazy finish to them, dropping like rocks in a pond. I struck out six, walked nobody, and missed the strike zone only twenty-two times over nine innings.

Ken Oberkfell, the Bisons' manager, who has been

around baseball for more than three decades, told the media afterward that it may have been the most dominant pitching performance he'd ever seen. The club owners rewarded us with a steak dinner the following night.

Of course, the prize I really wanted was a one-way ticket to Citi Field.

Five weeks into the season, my record was 4-2, my ERA 2.23. I'd struck out thirty-seven and walked eight. I was relaxing on one of my comfy air mattresses (I had my choice of air mattresses because Anne had taken the kids back to Nashville to finish the school year) when Ken Oberkfell called. "Sit tight," he said. "The Mets might be making a move."

Next thing I knew, I was in the outfield of Turner Field in Atlanta, throwing to bullpen catcher Dave Racaniello, with Dan Warthen observing. I was not scheduled to start against the Braves; Warthen just wanted to see me throw so he could figure out if he could use me. I didn't need any more than that for hope to kick in. Anne arranged for the kids to stay with her parents so she could meet me. We both knew this could very well be my last dance in The Show. Three months from then, I could have been in a college classroom.

Dan Warthen apparently liked what he saw, because I flew ahead of the team to Washington to get a full night's rest before our series against the Nationals. The equipment manager in the visitors' clubhouse issued me a gray road jersey with number 43 on the back.

Three hours before my first game as a New York Met, I felt acutely aware of how much I wanted to find a baseball home. I yearned to put down roots with a team and be a completely trustworthy performer, not a 4A guy who can pitch like Mr. Dependable one night and Lady Gaga the next.

After my pregame turkey sandwich in the players' lounge, I watched video of the Nationals with Dan, then spent some quiet time in prayer at my locker. I contemplated the fresh start ahead of me and suddenly all the old doubts and fears crept in:

Do you know how much pressure there is on you tonight? You know that if you stink, you're right back in Buffalo. What if you have another six-home-run game? How many more teams are going to give you a chance? This is your fifth organization in five years. Nothing is going to change just because your uniform does.

It was an insidious assault, but here's the switch: I didn't let it rock me.

Because of the work I'd done in counseling, I knew that though a bird of prey may fly into my head, I didn't have to let it build a nest there. I could say, "There's that bird again," and not give it any power.

Every athlete has fears and doubts. Those who say they don't are liars. The trick is that the best athletes have the anxious thoughts and brush them away like an umpire sweeps dirt off home plate.

When I took the mound in Nationals Park, I didn't want to hear this noise. I wanted to be fully present with my pitch, the way I learned to be after I came out of the Missouri.

The first batter I faced in my Mets career was Nyjer Morgan, the Nationals' center fielder. I went up on him 1-2 before throwing a knuckleball away. He surprised me, squaring around to bunt (with two strikes!). But he didn't deaden the ball enough, and it hung in the air for a little pop-up along the third-base line. I got a good break off the mound, but the ball was dropping fast. The only shot I had was to make a headlong dive. So I left my feet and laid myself out.

The ball landed in my glove. One out.

It was the perfect way to start. I love fielding my position. I love being an athlete. I'd always rather make a play like that than strike a guy out on three pitches.

After setting down the Nationals without a hit through three innings, our center fielder, Angel Pagan, gave us a lead with an inside-the-park home run in the top of the fourth. But the Nationals countered in the bottom of the inning, scoring twice on three singles, a walk, and a sacrifice fly.

In the fifth, I threw an ill-advised fastball to Livan Hernandez, a very good hitting pitcher, that he slapped into left for a single. Then I walked Nyjer Morgan. Two on and nobody out. A hit or two now and the floodgates could open. I probably wouldn't get out of the fifth. I could even find myself back on the inflatable mattress in the Snow Belt.

Cristian Guzmán, Washington's second baseman, stepped in. I expected a bunt. We all expected a bunt, so the corners came in. I got ahead 0-1 and, surprisingly, he didn't square. Maybe he didn't think he could get a bunt down on my knuckleball. On my second pitch I threw a good, spinless knuckleball that dropped late. Guzmán swung at it, looping it into center.

Pagan charged hard, kept charging, and reached down to make a gorgeous shoestring catch. Both runners thought the ball would drop in, so Angel hurried to get the ball to second for a force-out of Livan. But in his haste he airmailed it way over José Reyes's head, beyond the mound, which I had vacated to back up the plate. Catcher Henry Blanco alertly charged the ball and fired to Reyes at second. Reyes stepped on the bag for out two, then relayed the ball to Ike Davis at first for one of the oddest triple plays ever recorded.

An inning later, I got Pudge Rodriguez, my former Texas teammate, to hit into a weak, 6–4–3 double play. I came off the mound fired up, but the bullpen took over from there. I wound up with a no-decision in a 5–3 loss, but I'd given the Mets a quality start: two runs in six innings.

My first start at home came six days later, against the Phillies. School had ended, so Anne brought the kids to New York for the occasion, and we were all shoehorned into a hotel room near Times Square. As thrilled as I was for them to be near, I needed to make sure I got rest, and three kids under age nine in a hotel room is not necessarily conducive to sleeping in. I was way too cheap to spring for another room at $250 a night.

The day of the game, I kissed everybody good-bye and caught the subway to Queens, where the Mets' home, Citi Field, is located. The train trip helped me get into my game mind-set, and by the time I got to the park, I was tunneled in. I delivered again, pitching six shutout innings for my first National League victory.

For the next month I pitched better than I ever had in my entire big-league career. I was in an almost surreal groove, throwing as if each pitch might be the last of my life. Nothing could faze me.

After almost a week in the Times Square hotel, I learned an ex-Met, Shawn Green, had a condo in Connecticut we could use. We moved in, but apparently nobody told the management company, because not long after we arrived, the power was shut off. We lived in the dark, and the midsummer swelter, for five days. We loaded a foam cooler with ice for perishables, and got by with flashlights and candles. We could've moved somewhere else, gotten a hotel, but we didn't. I figured I was the only pitcher in Major League Baseball who went home to a dark house and read by candlelight after night games. Maybe I subconsciously wanted to relive my nomadic days when I slept in vacant houses.

In my own quirky way, I became a New York story—

an old knuckleballing guy with a Tennessee twang and a missing body part.

People kept waiting for me to revert to retread form, or for batters to figure out the "trick pitch" I throw. I had a career ERA of almost 5.00, after all.

That kind of talk didn't surprise or offend me. But it did make me want to change how people thought about the knuckleball, and how they thought about me. I wanted to demonstrate the degree to which change is possible, my own life being Exhibit A.

Once I was a hypercompetitive kid who threw in the mid-nineties. Now I was a hypercompetitive grown-up who dared hitters to get a piece of a flaky, fluttering ball I throw with my fingernails.

Once I kept secrets and hid and ran from the truth. Now I was about as close as anyone can get to being an open book.

Do you think it's a coincidence that when I was finally able to stop hiding as a human being, I also stopped hiding as a pitcher?

I don't.

Chapter 25

ENTER THE BAFFLER

July Fourth weekend, 2010, I took the Metro to Nationals Park. The subway car teemed with fans in red apparel, a smattering of jerseys with Ryan Zimmerman's number 11 and a slew of Stephen Strasburg T-shirts. I sat in the middle of the car, pretending to read *Life of Pi* by Yann Martel, but really eavesdropping on the banter. A little boy, maybe eight years old, on his way to his first ball game, fired questions at his father about Strasburg—and why wouldn't he? Strasburg was the most heralded pitching prospect in years, a kid who had single-handedly made a long-moribund franchise the talk of baseball, with his 100 mile per hour fastball and ridiculous curve.

I was eager to see him myself, because I was pitching against him that day. Could the contrast be starker? Young guy versus old guy, fireballer versus flutter-baller, Anointed One versus Anonymous One. Every great story needs tension, and this baseball narrative had it in abundance.

Nobody on the subway had any idea who I was—one of the perks of journeyman stature. I heard my name a dozen or more times and in a nearby seat a guy was reading an article from the *Wall Street Journal* headlined "Rocket Boy vs. The Baffler." The illustration with the story depicted Strasburg (aka Rocket Boy) as an airborne superhero in full costume, complete with chiseled physique and baseballs blazing out of his right hand. It depicted me (The Baffler) as a much less imposing figure, on the ground, with a question mark on my chest and baseballs floating all about.

I almost laughed out loud. The Baffler. I loved it.

"It's amazing that one guy can throw 100 [miles per hour] and the other can throw 75 and they can both be really good at what they do," David Wright said in the article.

Almost forty thousand people showed up for the game at Nationals Park, triple the turnout for my first start with the Mets, five weeks earlier. These people did not come out to see The Baffler.

We scored right away, on Jason Bay's RBI double in the top of the first. As I took the mound I was enthralled by the moment, and the challenge ahead. I relished that there was all this buzz around Strasburg, and that I was no more relevant than the right-field peanut vendor. I don't look like Stephen Strasburg, don't throw like him, and am certainly not as wealthy as young Mr. Strasburg, but I was ready to compete with him.

And I did precisely that.

Strasburg went five innings and gave up four hits and two runs. I went seven innings and gave up six hits and two unearned runs. Neither of us got the decision, although the Nationals got the win, rallying for four runs in the final two innings to go up 6–5. I wished the score was reversed, but I did my job, and did it well. I wished I had asked the guy on the subway if I could have his *Wall Street Journal* when he was finished with it. I really liked that cartoon.

We were ten games over .500 (47-37) and just two behind the Phillies in the National League East in early July, but we started to fade after the All-Star break. In mid-August, the Phillies came to Citi Field, giving us our last and best chance to get back in the race. I was coming off my worst start of the year, against the Phillies, in which I lasted just three innings and gave up eight hits and four earned runs in Citizens Bank Park. I wasn't quite as bad as the line sounds—there were some untimely bleeders and bloopers—but my team gave me a two-run lead against Roy Halladay in the first and I couldn't take care of it, and that was on me.

Now our rivals would be in our house. I got to the ballpark on Friday afternoon for my start and found myself in a surprisingly good place. I wasn't panicky because I'd had a bad outing. I had not lost faith in my knuckleball, or let birds of prey feather their nests in my head.

Every year I've thrown the knuckleball, it has gotten more consistent, with more finish, so consequently I have more confidence in it. In 2008 in Seattle, about 65 percent of my pitches were knuckleballs. In 2009, in Minnesota, about 75 percent were knuckleballs. This year I was throwing knuckleballs 85 percent of the time, which is how it should be. It is, after all, my best pitch, my best chance to win. I was also effectively changing speeds, throwing knuckleballs as slow as 69 miles per hour and as hard as 81. I chose to focus on my body of work with the Mets, and not one shabby start in Citizens Bank Park.

There is a blank canvas before me tonight, I told myself. It's up to me to paint it, to dab enough nasty knuckle-balls in enough good spots to make it come together.

If I work the brush with full conviction, maybe I can make it a masterpiece.

I thanked God for this newfound ability to shake off the memories of my previous start and take the mound that night as a free man. My opponent was Cole Hamels. It wasn't going to be easy.

Hamels and I matched zeroes through five. I got through the fourth inning on nine pitches and had yet to give up a hit. In the fifth, Jayson Werth, the Phillies right fielder, led off. Werth had success against me before; he's a dangerous guy. The count ran full after five straight knuckleballs. Henry Blanco, my catcher, called for a fastball.

I took a step back and looked in again at Henry. Why was he calling for fastball? If Werth waited on it, our scoreless tie would be gone in the time it took for the ball to clear the outfield wall.

I shook him off, but Henry put down the fastball sign again. In my typical start, there were only three or four times a game when we deviated from the knuckleball-intensive game plan. This was one of them. Henry is an astute guy and he must've seen something in how Werth was holding his hands or how he had moved up in the box to get the knuckleball early. I trusted him.

I wound up and delivered a fastball on the outer half of the plate—a defrost pitch, as I call it, because you throw slow, slow, slow, and then you heat it up in a hurry. Werth was completely defrosted. He didn't move a muscle.

Strike three.

One out.

Next I got Shane Victorino swinging on a knuckleball, and Brian Schneider, who grounded out weakly. Halfway through, and I still had a no-hitter, although our bats hadn't gotten to Hamels, either.

I got the first out in the sixth and then Hamels stepped in. I started him off with a knuckleball, which he lined into right for a single, ending my no-hit fantasy. The Citi Field crowd recognized the effort with a warm ovation.

I still had work to do. I got Jimmy Rollins to ground out and retired Plácido Polanco on a long fly to center.

In the bottom of the sixth, Carlos Beltrán hit an RBI double that gave us a 1–0 lead. Now I needed to make it hold up. I sat down the middle of the order on eight pitches in the seventh, and needed only nine to get three fly-ball outs in the eighth.

As I warmed up for the ninth, three outs away from

a one-hit shutout, I had another one of my epiphanies: For the first time in my big-league career, I felt dominant. The way I was controlling the pitch, the consistency of my feel and my release point, the sharpness of its movement—it all made for a knuckleball that was just a beast to get a good piece of.

Domonic Brown came up first, pinch-hitting for Hamels. On an 0-1 pitch he grounded out to short. Rollins, next, did the same thing, only he hit it to Ike Davis at first.

Polanco was up, the last man between me and a shutout of the National League champions. The fans stood and started clapping, encouraging me to shut the door firmly. Polanco took a knuckleball for a strike and then I threw one that darted away from him. He swung anyway and hit it off the end of his bat, a harmless fly to right field. Jeff Francoeur squeezed it, and my day at the office—and my first shutout in seven years—was complete.

Henry Blanco and the rest of the team rushed up to congratulate me, and the Citi Field crowd stood in appreciation. More than anything, I felt grateful for the opportunity God gave me to shine and for feeling as though I just might belong there.

As I walked into the clubhouse, I had a flashback to my only other major-league shutout, in Comerica Park against the Tigers. I was pitching for the Rangers and Alex Rodriguez was the shortstop. A-Rod came up to me after the game. "You have me to thank for that," he said.

"What do you mean?" I asked.

"I called every pitch from shortstop," A-Rod said, explaining that he relayed signs to our catcher that day, Einar Diaz.

"Well, thank you," I told A-Rod.

The next time out, I gave up six hits and six earned runs in a 9–2 loss to the Royals.

I asked A-Rod after the game if I had him to thank for that too. "No, I didn't call the pitches tonight," he said.

We stayed over .500 until the middle of September, but a 5-10 finish in the final fifteen games consigned us to fourth place in the National League East and a 79-83 record. Even though we were out of the pennant race, each start was important to me because I was still a pitcher without a contract for the following year. I'd been a vagabond for a long time and I wanted a home.

The only way that would happen was if I proved to the Mets they needed me. I accomplished that by finishing strong, treating every start as if it were my own personal game seven, no matter what the standings said.

My last start of the year was against the Milwaukee Brewers, in the second game of a doubleheader at Citi Field. I went seven innings, gave up six hits and one run, and took the loss. I finished the year with an 11-9 record and a 2.84 ERA. It was the most victories I'd had in a season, and the lowest ERA I'd had in a season by far. I hoped it was good enough for the Mets to re-up me for a year through the arbitration process, but when talks began between Bo McKinnis and the Mets, it quickly became clear that a two-year agreement was within reach. I wound up agreeing to a deal for $7.8 million over two years.

There was only one downside to it.

I had to get a physical, my first full baseball physical since the one I had with Dr. Conway in 1996—the one that launched me on the road to orthopedic infamy, and cost me my first-round offer.

"It's going to be okay," Bo said, trying to reassure me. "There's absolutely nothing wrong with you. It's going to be routine."

Bo joined me at the hospital and stayed for the

ninety minutes it took to have my arm checked out, undergo an MRI and a variety of other tests.

I wanted to believe it was going to be fine, but didn't I think that in 1996?

Yes, I did.

This time, everything checked out fine.

I felt immediate and immense relief. I may have been well short of the Jeter/A-Rod income bracket, but the contract I was about to sign was ten times the amount I lost when the Rangers retracted their offer. It seemed miraculous to me, the grace of God at work in my life again.

And with a fourth child on the way, the timing was good.

But the greatest relief was to be wanted. I didn't have to go through a dog and pony show to convince a team I was better than my numbers. I didn't have to prove anything—because I'd already done it, across 174 innings and 27 starts. And that meant, for the first time in fifteen years, I did not have to go to spring training to audition for a job.

I already had a job.

I belonged.

Chapter 26

A PLACE TO PARK MYSELF

I t took the better part of two decades, but when I arrived in Port St. Lucie, Florida, for spring training in February 2011, I had my very own parking spot. Number 43 was stenciled right on the asphalt between two white lines in the players' lot, not far from Frankie Rodriguez's number 62 and his black Lamborghini. I rode a bicycle to the park most days, but that misses the point: I was no longer just some guy passing through, living on the minor-league fringe.

I belonged there.

Right from the start, 2011 was not about just surviving. I wanted more. I wanted to prove myself trustworthy not just as a pitcher but also as a husband and a father and a believer.

Trust was a big issue around the Mets, for reasons that went far beyond one pitcher's soul-searching. We had a new general manager, Sandy Alderson, and a new manager, Terry Collins, but the headlines all spring were about the Mets being on the brink of financial ruin after being defrauded of hundreds of millions of dollars by financier Bernie Madoff.

The wreckage Madoff left behind was unfathomable—lives ruined, families wiped out—but neither the scandal nor its possible impact on the Mets was ever mentioned to us, the players. Some black ballplayer humor—which is as old as the game itself—surfaced from time to time: Maybe we'll be staying at Motel 6s on the road this year. Or: I hope they didn't invest our meal money with Bernie.

Not having to pitch my way onto the team freed me to experiment, so I worked on a super-slow knuckleball. I throw most of my knuckleballs between 75 and 80 miles per hour. Dan Warthen and I agreed that throwing the pitch at 60 miles per hour might be a very effective weapon. The challenge was disguising the release so I had the element of surprise. It took several weeks to get to the point that I could use it in a game.

We drove south when camp ended: Our first series of the year was against Miami. I was pumped to start the third game of the season. Of course, the noise in my head started up again, fears that I wouldn't be good enough, and that I'd be back in Buffalo. There was an extra layer of pressure this year—proving myself worthy of my new contract.

I also felt pressure to stuff socks in the mouths of all the baseball pundits who wrote or said my success in 2010 was a fluke.

As I prepared to face the Marlins, I didn't try to eliminate the fear or the pressure so much as to acknowledge it before consigning it to the trash can.

I asked God to let me compete as a man with the faith to rise above whatever fear I might have and to put everything I have into every pitch I throw.

I pitched six innings, gave up no earned runs, and struck out seven. We won, 9–2.

The noise in my head was a nonfactor.

I wanted to belong and the Mets delivered in a big way, configuring the rotation so that I could start the home opener at Citi Field against the Nationals, an incredible honor. When I was introduced before the game, I got a loud ovation. When you've had more boos than cheers in your career, you notice big ovations, believe me.

It was a raw April day, maybe forty-five degrees at

game time, but my knuckleball was moving all over the place as I warmed up. Cold? Nah, it was a beautiful day for baseball.

After getting two quick outs in the top of the first, I threw an 80 mile an hour knuckleball to Ryan Zimmerman. The moment it left my hand, I knew I had a problem. I had broken the nail of my right index finger. The pressure of the nail against the ball caused the nail to split. A broken nail is a disaster for a knuckleball pitcher. If a nail is broken, I can't grip the ball right, and bad things ensue.

The count against Zimmerman was 2-2, and I didn't want to risk making the nail worse, so I threw one of my new, super-slow, 59 mile per hour numbers.

Zimmerman was ahead of it, by about a half hour. He missed it by so much, he laughed.

I did not laugh.

Between innings, I worked feverishly on my nail. Mike Herbst, our assistant trainer, kept my nail-repair kit in his trainers' box. My kit includes all the indispensable tools of the knuckleballing trade: a glass file (metal files can leave jagged edges), superglue, a tube of acrylic, and a buffer.

I tried to even out the nail with the file. Then I applied a hardening agent called Trind Nail Repair that my mother-in-law gave me. I could dab on Trind until Bernie Madoff got out of jail, but it wasn't going to address the central issue: The broken nail was too short to allow me to grip my knuckleball.

This was trouble with a capital *T*.

In the second, I got two fly-ball outs, but Rick Ankiel singled and I walked the next two hitters on five pitches apiece. I'd never broken a nail during a game before. I tried to gut through it, but I had that old familiar feeling of facing major-league hitters with a peashooter. To throw a knuckleball without the nail on my index finger is like a quarterback trying to throw a pass without his pinkie.

The bases were loaded and I went up 0-2 on the opposing pitcher, Jordan Zimmermann. One pitch away from getting out of it, I threw a mediocre knuckleball and Zimmermann drove it into right for a two-run single. I was furious at myself, at the situation.

At the end of the inning, I took off my glove and slammed it against the dugout wall in disgust. I had such high expectations for this start.

I issued three more walks, one with the bases loaded, and left the game after five. We lost, 6–2. I felt completely humbled and deflated.

Opening day. Check.

Huge ovation. Check.

Broken nail. Checkmate.

I didn't even make it into the sixth inning.

I spent the next few days obsessing over my busted nail. I took calcium supplements and reapplied my mother-in-law's nail goo. Two days before my next start, the nail was growing nicely and I went to the bullpen for my scheduled throwing session. Halfway through, the nail split again. Blood spurted all over my right hand.

This time the split was all the way down to the nail bed.

Now, basically, I had no nail. If I went out there against the Rockies without a fingernail, I'd get raked. I told Dan Warthen I needed to get to a nail salon ASAP. The words weren't out of my mouth when I realized how ridiculous they sounded. Imagine Clayton Kershaw or Justin Verlander rushing up to their pitching coaches: "Emergency! I need a manicure!"

"Go," Dan said.

I asked him not to tell Terry. I didn't want people getting worked up about it.

A few minutes later I headed to the parking lot with Theresa Corderi, one of our clubhouse cooks. She knows

Queens and she knows nails. She took me to a little place on College Point Boulevard called Pink Nails, run by some lovely Korean ladies.

Do I have to tell you I was the only ballplayer, in full uniform, on the premises?

For seven bucks (tip included), I got acrylic slathered onto to my one busted nail. It seemed to adhere well. Theresa and I hustled back to Citi Field. As we pulled in, I saw Jeff Wilpon, the Mets' chief operating officer, just ahead of us. I prayed he wouldn't turn around and see me arriving at the ballpark ten minutes before game time. I wondered if I should've gotten a note from the people at Pink Nails if I needed backup, but it didn't come to that. Jeff kept walking.

My nail held up okay against the Rockies, but that's about all that held up. Every time out so far that season, something went wrong. Balls found gaps. I surrendered home runs when I couldn't afford to. The games where I pitched well and the team played well never seemed to align.

I went into my ninth start of the year, in Houston, with a 1-5 record and a 4.50 ERA. I was embarrassed by the numbers next to my name. This was my chance to do something about it. Domed stadiums are usually good for knuckleballs.

Michael Bourn led off for the Astros. He mashed the third pitch of the game, a 2-0 fastball, for a triple to right center. Hunter Pence singled. Carlos Lee singled. Followed by three more hits to the next three hitters. It was raining singles. Inside a dome!

One inning and I was already down four runs. I pleaded with Terry Collins to leave me in, to at least eat some innings and save the bullpen. I pitched into the sixth. By the end of my outing, my ERA had gone up, not down.

I left the mound trying to channel my inner Greg Maddux, who once said, "The best pitchers have a short-term memory and a bulletproof confidence."

Easier said than done. I was frustrated beyond belief, not just because of my horrible record, but because I knew I was close. My knuckleball was moving well. I just seemed to make a bad pitch at precisely the wrong moment.

After the game, I got a text from Anne. She attached two adorable photos of Van, our seven-week-old boy, to cheer me up. The media was waiting to talk to me about my debacle. No doubt numerous stories were being drafted about my fairy dust running out. Let them write whatever they wanted. Somehow, even as I stood at my locker after a wretched performance, I felt more centered than I ever had. I trusted myself, that I was close to turning things around on the mound. Life was good. God was so merciful. A rocky start in a baseball game could not change that.

Baseball can be a brutal business. Your failures are right there illuminated on the scoreboard, whether it's a .182 batting average or a 5.08 ERA. The numbers go viral on the Internet, giving everybody and their aunt Bessie a chance to weigh in on your deficiencies. I'm pretty good at not taking it personally. Much worse for me was what my shabby numbers meant: I hadn't been someone my team could count on. An ERA of 5.08 meant I hadn't given my team much of a chance to win. There were variables beyond my control that inflate an ERA, like outfield misadventures and bloops that fell in, but that stuff tends to even out.

More than my won-lost record, I care about my ERA. If you gave me a choice between being 12-10 with a 4.25 ERA and 10-2 with a 2.75 ERA, I'll take the latter. It's not because I don't want my team to win as many games as possible, but because if I have an ERA of under 3.00 it means in the long run we're going to win a lot more games than if I'm giving up an extra run and a half.

So after a brutal April, I went into ERA-reduction mode as the team tried to scrape its way into contention with the Phillies and Braves. My next time out, I beat the Yankees at Yankee Stadium, giving up four hits and a run over six innings.

On to Chicago, to play the Cubs. I racked up two quick scoreless innings to start and had two outs and two on. Kosuke Fukudome was at the plate and I got him to hit a roller toward second. I broke off the mound to cover first. Halfway there I felt a pain in my foot and did a face plant onto the grass at Wrigley Field. It felt as if somebody had driven a railroad spike through my right arch. I knew immediately my day had ended. The question quickly became: Is it worse than one abbreviated outing?

I limped back to New York on crutches to see a foot specialist who had bad news for me: I'd partially torn my plantar fascia, a band of tissue that runs along the bottom of the foot. The treatment was rest. When it didn't hurt, I could pitch again.

Hmm, I thought.

When Jonathon Niese or Dillon Gee or any other young guy asked me for advice, one of the first things I told them was: "Don't go on the disabled list if you can avoid it. I've seen people get Wally Pipped more times than I can count."

Wally Pipp was the Yankees' first baseman in 1925. He came to the ballpark with a horrific headache one day, and asked the trainer for aspirin. The manager overheard his request and let him have the day off. "We'll try that kid Gehrig today," the manager said.

Lou Gehrig played the next 2,130 games at first. Pipp never got his job back. In 1926, the Yankees traded him to Cincinnati. He was later quoted as saying, "I took the two most expensive aspirin in history."

As I sat on the examining table, I remembered my own advice. The last thing I wanted was to give the Mets any reason to look for a replacement. I could deal with pain.

The doctor poked my foot. "Does this hurt?" he asked. I shook my head. Then he moved down my foot a bit and pressed hard. "How about this?"

"Not much," I answered, lying. I am an accomplished liar when it comes to staying off the DL. In a game against the Cardinals a bit later in the season, David Freese hit me in the neck with a line drive. I picked up the ball and threw him out at first. As soon as I came off the mound, our trainer, Ray Ramirez, looked for damage. "Did that get you?" he asked.

I'd be out of the game if he knew I took a line drive in the neck. "It got a piece of my glove," I said. "I'm fine."

He was suspicious (I'm not the only major leaguer who will do anything to avoid the DL), so he checked the replay, but it wasn't clear-cut whether it hit my neck or my glove. I stayed in the game.

After the foot injury, I got almost round-the-clock treatment from Ray—ultrasound, heat, ice, a whirlpool. Our massage therapist went at the underside of my right foot hard. It hurt a ton, but my foot felt much better for it. The treatments were working. Three days later, I told Dan Warthen I wanted to throw my usual bullpen session. He was surprised, but he liked the way I threw.

"I need to see you field your position," he then demanded, rolling a series of balls out to see how well I could get off the mound. I got off okay. Not great, but okay.

"I'm good to go," I assured him.

Five days after going splat on the Wrigley grass, I had convinced the Mets to let me make my next start against the Pirates at Citi Field. Ray gave me an injection of Toradol, a painkiller and anti-inflammatory, an hour before first pitch. I'd never taken anything stronger than Advil before getting on the mound, but my foot was still barking at me. I got the shot in the butt, and it made a big difference.

I didn't make another start the rest of the year without Toradol.

Against the Pirates, I took a two-hit shutout and a 1–0 lead into the eighth, only to see it dissolve on a two-out, two-run single by Neil Walker. I struck out a career-high ten hitters and threw eighty-one strikes and only twenty-seven balls.

I took the loss and fell to 2-6. Not the outcome I had in mind, but I felt good about my effort.

Effort, it occurred to me later that night, was really what mattered most, wasn't it? Outcomes are dependent on a lot of things outside your own control. But you honor yourself and your game when you pour all you have into it, when you live in the athletic moment. I will never have the weaponry of Tim Lincecum or C. C. Sabathia, but I can give just as much of myself. I can compete as hard, or harder. It's the lesson Uncle Ricky kept pounding into me as a kid: The mental is to the physical as four is to one.

Without putting it so succinctly, my mother taught me the same thing: You do not pout or mope or pass blame when things don't go your way. If you have a problem, find a solution. If you make a mistake, look in the mirror. If your car breaks down after picking up your toddler from day care and you get attacked by a dog, you make sure the baby is safe and you keep walking.

Baseball, for me, is a game of managing regrets. You are always going to have regrets; they are as much a part of baseball as home plate. If you let your regrets linger, they will devour you. Remember Greg Maddux's words: You need a short memory. You manage your regrets by letting them go, taking them to the curb as if they were the trash.

You manage them by forgetting them as soon as the ball leaves your hand, and turning 100 percent of your intensity to the next pitch. It's the only pitch you can still throw, after all.

As the 2011 season wound down, I felt good about my work and how I'd managed my regrets, of which there were, unfortunately, no shortage. I regretted my lack of feel for my knuckleball early on, my tendency to give up home runs in big spots, my putrid start that pushed my ERA over 5.00.

I could easily have let those things turn my season into a train wreck, but I didn't, and that constituted progress. In the twenty-four starts I made after the debacle in Houston, I won only six times, but I'd gotten my ERA down to 2.60—one of the best ERAs in the league over that span. I had a streak of eleven straight quality starts, dating to July.

Now I had one more, my last start of the season, in the first game of a doubleheader against the Phillies at Citi Field. The Phillies had the division locked up and we had the off-season locked up, so theoretically the game meant nothing.

Except to me. It meant plenty to me.

After I got my last shot of Toradol in my butt—I wouldn't miss those in the off-season—I sat at my locker in a back corner of the clubhouse. I felt sad about the season ending. I would turn thirty-seven in October, and even though every member of the Jedi Council of Knuckleballers pitched into their forties, I realized I was closer to the end of my career than the beginning. I was proud of how hard we battled as a team that year, even when we had more Buffalo Bisons on the field than New York Mets. I understood management's decision to trade Carlos Beltrán from a business standpoint, but, from a competitor's standpoint, it's tough to lose one of your best players when you're vying for a pennant. So I was melancholy about the season ending, but determined to finish strong. Isn't that what people remember? How you finish?

I prayed to God, and gave thanks for the many ways He blessed me that year. Then I went out to pitch.

Jimmy Rollins led off for the Phillies. I threw two knuckleballs to go up 0-2, then froze him with my 61 mile per hour slowpoke. One out. I wound up retiring the side in order, and doing the same in the second.

And the third.

And the fourth.

By the time I got John Mayberry Jr. to hit a foul pop, I'd faced fifteen Phillies and retired fifteen Phillies.

The crowd cheered as I walked off. A no-hitter through five. When you're more than halfway through, you start to hope.

When I had the one-hitter against the Phillies in 2010, it was their pitcher Cole Hamels who broke it up in the sixth. He was my adversary again that day. I kept that in mind when I went out for the sixth inning. Carlos Ruiz, the Phillies' catcher, led off. I quickly went up 0-2, but he worked the count full. He fouled off the next three knucklers, then I threw ball four. It didn't miss by much, but it missed.

That was it for the perfect game, but I couldn't dwell on that if I wanted to win.

I got the next two guys and then Rollins was at the

plate again. On the 1-1 pitch, he belted a knuckleball deep to right, way back. Nick Evans scrambled back to the track, got turned around, and somehow made a tumbling catch on the warning track. The crowd went berserk. I punched the air.

Thank you, Nick.

No Mets pitcher had ever thrown a no-hitter in the team's fifty seasons of existence, a span of nearly eight thousand games. It was one of the more bizarre streaks in the history of the game. Everybody in the ballpark was aware of that, including me. With Nick's play in right and the knuckleball I had going, I allowed myself to think this could be the game.

Plácido Polanco grounded out to open the seventh. Next up was Shane Victorino, a switch-hitter who had taken to batting right-handed against me after having so little success from the left side of the plate. I fired a knuckleball for a strike, then he looked at ball one. I tried another knuckler. It felt good leaving my hand, but it didn't drop. Victorino turned on it, crushing a line drive to left. Nobody was catching this one. It went for a double.

The crowd stood and cheered me, for a good while.

I gave myself a few moments to be sad about losing the no-hitter, then turned my attention to Ryan Howard. On my first offering, Howard bounced a ball up the middle, scoring Victorino. Two batters, two hits, and the no-hitter and shutout were both gone. Not only that, but now I was on the hook for a loss.

In the bottom of the inning, pinch hitter Val Pascucci, just up from the minors, drove a home run over the left-field fence to tie the game. The dugout exploded, euphoric that we'd finally broken through. But I was scheduled to hit that inning too, so Terry put Ronny Paulino in to hit for me, hoping to scratch out another run. I was done for the day, but at least I wouldn't get my fourteenth loss.

David Wright took care of business in the eighth, smacking a double that scored Ruben Tejada with the game-winning run.

We won the second game of the doubleheader too.

It's all about how you finish, right?

Chapter 27

JUDGMENT DAY

2012 was two weeks old and I was reading a sign that said: **CONGRATULATIONS! YOU'RE NOW AT UHURU PEAK.** That is the top of Mt. Kilamanjaro, the highest mountain in Africa. I climbed this mountain to raise money for an organization that aids homeless and abused teenaged girls in India.

By the time I returned to sea level, and to Port St. Lucie, I had put the majesty of an African sunrise atop Mt. Kilimanjaro behind me. I had a much more pressing issue before me.

The first version of this book you are reading was published for adults in March 2012, and as you know now, it revealed secrets I'd kept my whole career, and most of my life.

In the weeks before publication, the Mets organization worried that I might have taken shots at them in the book, or told unseemly tales from the locker room. I assured them that the only person I threw under the bus was me. The day before the book was officially released, the Mets publicity department distributed copies to the beat writers who cover the team. Stories started showing up on the Internet. *Sports Illustrated* published an article, along with a short excerpt from the book. ESPN aired a segment on me. Much of the focus, not surprisingly, was on my admission that I'd been sexually abused as a kid.

Now it's all out there, I told myself. There was no going back, even if I wanted to, which I didn't. I didn't write the book to make money or headlines. I wrote it because I needed to, because it helped me and I hoped it could help other people, who might be running from their own past, weighed down by their own toxic secrets.

I walked into the clubhouse the day after the stories appeared, deeply anxious about what the response would be. I tried not to be self-conscious, but that was a lost cause. I said hello to a few guys and headed to my locker to get changed. It seemed like any other day. If I was getting strange looks, I didn't see them. Dillon Gee, one locker over, greeted me warmly and didn't ask to be relocated. I felt tremendous relief.

A few minutes later I ran into our owner, Fred Wilpon, in the clubhouse. Fred was not a frequent visitor to the clubhouse. He moved close to me in a way he never had before. He gave me a hug and cupped my chin in his hand.

"This is a story that needs to be told and I'm very proud of you for telling it," he said.

"Thank you, Fred," I said.

I breathed a deep sigh of relief.

Chapter 28

AN ALL-STAR SEASON

My first start of 2012 came in our second game of the year, against the Braves at Citi Field. Johan Santana was superb on opening day, his first start back from major arm surgery. That gave the whole club a big emotional boost, and now I wanted to keep it going. But the noise was back, on cue, ready to pound me:

You know what's going to happen if you don't get off to a strong start this season? People are going to write that it's because of the book. They're going to say that you are distracted. That you've opened your life up to intense scrutiny and can't deal with it.

Here I was again, consumed with proving myself once more. I got to the park late morning. I asked God for strength, and the clarity to block out the noise and pour everything into the moment.

Throw the best knuckleball you can. Get the ball back from Josh Thole, and then throw another one. That was my mantra and it worked. I had a good, if not spectacular, outing—giving up five hits and two runs over six innings. Though I walked four batters, I pitched out of trouble effectively, except for a two-run homer Martin Prado hit in the fifth. We won, 4–2. Everybody went home happy.

In my next start against Cliff Lee and the Phillies, I had a 4–1 lead in the top of the fifth. I came up to the plate and hit a dribbler to Jimmy Rollins at short. I was busting it down the line when I felt a painful tug in the lower part of my abdomen. I got thrown out, but my bigger concern was the tug. I was pretty sure I'd torn a muscle.

In keeping with my I-won't-be-Wally-Pipped mentality, I kept the information about the tug and the possible tear to myself.

My abdomen was sore, but I let adrenaline override the pain, pitching seven innings and giving up one run. We won again.

After the game I confided in Ray Ramirez, our trainer. He looked me over and confirmed my self-diagnosis. The injury lingered the whole year, but I dealt with it by resuming the shots of Toradol before each start. A true pain in my butt.

I got lit up in my next start in Atlanta, where it was raining so hard, I felt like I was throwing water balloons, but I won three of my next four starts to go to 5-1. By the time we got to Pittsburgh for my start against the Pirates in late May at PNC Park, I not only had worries about how my book would be received behind me, I had a new-fangled variation on my knuckleball.

Dan Warthen and I had been working on throwing a knuckler that gave the illusion of rising as it got to the plate. It really stayed on the same plane, but if guys were missing it, I didn't care if nobody figured that out. I didn't change my grip at all, but I shortened my stride and stayed under the ball a little more. It gave hitters one more thing to think about, and made the pitch that much harder to track. The early returns against the Pirates were striking. I gave up one run in seven innings and struck out eleven without issuing a single base-on-balls. I can't tell you for sure how many times guys swung and missed at the pseudo-riser, but I was sure I was going to keep throwing it.

I struck out ten more and walked just one in my next start, pitching no-run, three-hit ball into the eighth inning against the Padres.

By now there was no doubt I was pitching the best baseball of my life. Probably the single biggest reason for it was that I was controlling my knuckleball to a degree I didn't know was possible, given the erratic nature of the pitch. I spent the first two months of the 2012 season ahead in the count. Against the Pirates, for example, I threw 89 pitches, 68 of them strikes. When you are always around the plate, it changes the whole balance of the at-bat. Hitters can't go up there and say, "I'm going to wait until I get a better count, and make him throw me something I can hit." Now if they waited, they were likely looking at being in an 0-2 hole. That changed everything, and put me in command. It was an exhilarating feeling.

The reigning World Series champions, the St. Louis Cardinals, came to Citi Field the first weekend in June. We were not intimidated, posting our own impressive 28-23 record at the time, keeping pace with the leaders in the NL East and surprising all the wise guys who predicted we'd start in the cellar and dwell there all year.

Johan was on the mound for the opener of the series, and he'd been pitching great. He pitched great that night too, taking a no-hitter to the ninth. By that time, we were ahead 5–0, and the tension had become so great, I simply could not watch. I put a towel over my head in the dugout, knowing the sounds the fans made would tell me if it was okay to look.

Johan got the first two guys out. One more out to go.

The crowd was on its feet. Of course, the next batter

could not be some slouch with a propensity to hit weak grounders to an infielder. That would've been too easy.

No, up stepped David Freese, MVP of the 2011 World Series. He did not go quietly, working the count full. My towel was still in place.

Johan threw a sinking changeup.

Freese swung.

Freese missed.

Citi Field detonated with joy, fifty-plus years of no-hit history obliterated. I snapped the towel off and charged the mound with the rest of the team.

It was an unforgettable moment, for the franchise and for my teammate, a champion of a competitor. It was only later, when the celebration died down, that I remembered: *I have to follow this act, eighteen hours from now.*

A daunting task, but I was determined not to let anything disrupt the rhythm I was in. I didn't throw a no-hitter, but I did shut out the Cardinals on seven hits to run my record to 8-1. I struck out nine and walked nobody. Of the 100 pitches I threw, 73 of them were strikes.

Who knew I was just getting started?

In my next three starts, I gave up no earned runs. I pitched back-to-back one-hitters against the Rays and the Orioles, striking out twenty-five and walking two. In fact, no one had scored a run on me in more than forty innings. My record went to 11-1.

Suddenly, happily, my pitching world had spun into an orbit that is usually the domain of Cy Young winners and Hall of Famers.

Nobody could believe it. A knuckleball pitcher—the only one left after Tim Wakefield's retirement—was leading the league in strikeouts? Writers kept asking me how I was able to control a famously unruly pitch, how I was getting such results. I didn't want to engage in excruciating analysis. Truly, I didn't want to do any analysis at all. I wanted to keep the mind-set: Live one pitch at a time.

I had been getting progressively better at throwing the knuckleball. Throwing it at different speeds, different elevations, throwing most everything for strikes. I can't say I knew this was coming, but I knew I was getting better with my knuckleball every year, and now, in 2012, I was in a whole new place altogether.

What's not to like about that?

In late June we played the Yankees on ESPN's *Sunday Night Baseball*, C. C. Sabathia vs. R. A. Dickey, Yankee ace vs. Met upstart, The Big Man vs. The Baffler. I had not given up an earned run since the Pirates game on May 22. The streak was a cool thing and I hoped it would go to a hundred innings, but it also weighed on my mind, in part because I had to constantly answer questions about it, and about whether I thought I could match or surpass Orel Hershiser's record of fifty-nine scoreless innings. For a guy who had spent his whole professional life being overlooked, it was a little over-whelming. Part of me wished I could find a way to keep pitching at this level, but do it without attention.

Alas, that is not how it works.

Neither C.C. nor I was very good on *Sunday Night Baseball*. My scoreless-innings streak ended at forty-four and a third innings when my buddy from my Rangers days, Mark Teixeira, hit a sacrifice fly in the third. Then Nick Swisher belted a three-run homer off me. I wound up giving up five runs in six innings, but our bats rallied to get me off the hook for the loss.

I returned to form against the Dodgers in L.A. five days later, pitching three-hit, scoreless ball over eight innings and striking out ten. My record was now at 12-1. *If this is a dream,* I was thinking, *please don't wake me.*

Two days later the phone rang in my hotel room at nine a.m. The caller was our general manager, Sandy Alderson.

"Congratulations. You were voted to the All-Star team. You deserve it," Sandy said.

It took a minute to wrap my head around this news. There aren't many first-time All-Stars who are thirty-seven years old. To get this sort of affirmation meant so much.

The New York media found a tempest in All-Star team manager Tony La Russa's teapot when La Russa chose San Francisco Giant pitcher Matt Cain to start the game over me, but his choice didn't cost me any sleep. Sure, I'd love to be the starting pitcher in the All-Star game. Who wouldn't? With a 12-1 record and a 2.40 ERA, I had the credentials to start, but not getting the call was not going to spoil the experience of going to Kansas City and being a part of the greatest assemblage of baseball players in the world. The best part was being able to share the experience with Anne and the kids. We all rode in the back of a Chevy truck for the All-Star Game Parade through Kansas City's Country Club Plaza. Little Eli had a baseball and he waved it to the fans lining the parade route, holding it with his knuckleball grip, of course.

I got a big cheer when I was introduced before the game. When La Russa called for me to pitch the bottom of the sixth, I ran in from the pen and I listened to the cheers. The field looked brighter and greener than any I'd ever seen—maybe even more vivid than Safeco green. I looked to where Anne, the kids, and my mom were sitting and I felt almost as if I was on stage at a Broadway musical. My contribution lasted only fifteen pitches, but I savored throwing every one of them. I retired the side by getting Miguel Cabrera, a man who at the end of the season would win baseball's first Triple Crown since 1967, to hit into a 6–4–3 double play.

I walked off the mound thinking: Only God could write a story like this one.

Chapter 29

A SUMMIT I NEVER THOUGHT I'D REACH

Things unraveled for the Mets in the second half (again), and gloom descended on Citi Field as we sank in the standings. I wasn't as dominant in the second half either, but when I shut out the Marlins on the last day of August, my record was 17-4, and I was determined to get to twenty wins. I didn't deliberately try to make things as dramatic as they possibly could be, but I split my next four decisions, and wound up taking the mound at Citi Field for the very last home game of the year with a record of 19-6.

The opponent was the Pirates. After retiring the side in order in the first, maybe my nerves got to me. For sure the Pirates got to me, and I gave up two runs in the second. Uh-oh.

No worries: My teammates had my back. In fact, it seemed like everybody at Citi Field that day was working, collectively, toward that twentieth win. In the bottom of the second, Ike Davis said, effectively, "I got this, R.A.," and homered to get back one of the runs I gave up.

The Pirates were out of contention too, but they are major-league ballplayers with their own pride, and they played with a determination to deprive me of that elusive twentieth victory. I would expect nothing less from them. In the top of the fourth, ex-Met Rod Barajas took me deep to push the Pittsburgh lead to 3–1.

My guys answered with singles from Daniel Murphy, David Wright, and Scott Hairston to narrow the gap to 3–2. This had to be one of the tensest September games ever played between two clubs long out of the pennant race. At least, that's what it felt like to me. The fans were totally into it too. If you had wandered into Citi Field from Tatooine on September 27, 2012, you would definitely be right to assume that something big was at stake.

I issued a walk in the top of the fifth, but I tucked it into the middle of a hat trick of strikeouts. No harm, no foul.

In the bottom of the fifth, Pirates pitcher Kevin Correia gave up a free pass himself, putting Andres Torres at first. I tried to help my own cause, but struck out swinging. No matter. Ruben Tejada singled. Daniel Murphy did the same, scoring Torres. Tie game.

In the dugout, I exhaled with relief.

Then Wright, who had been just tremendous all year, gave the whole stadium a chance to unclench their shoulders and relax a bit when he crushed a three-run homer that put us up 6–3.

Getting the lead refueled my tank. I recorded five straight outs on strikeouts in one stretch. I got Andrew McCutcheon to hit a deep, but harmless, fly to center to end the seventh, and thought: I'm done. But Terry Collins encouraged me to go out for the eighth. I located some reserves I didn't know I had and struck out Garrett Jones and Pedro Alvarez.

Now I really did have nothing left, but the bullpen was ready. When I walked Travis Snider in an eight-pitch battle, Terry emerged from the dugout. I'd thrown 128 pitches, given up nine hits, and struck out thirteen. The crowd had been chanting my name intermittently throughout the game. Now they stood as I walked toward the dugout, pouring so much emotion and affection into me, I wanted to cry with happiness.

I tipped my hat but wished I could do more. I wanted to remember this moment forever, and I will. I watched the rest of the game in the dugout, except I didn't really watch. I just peeked from time to time, because I couldn't bear the tension. The bullpen wobbled and our lead narrowed to 6–5. The atmosphere at Citi Field shifted back to pins-and-needles mode, as if all thirty thousand fans were holding their breath together. It wasn't the same historic moment as Johan's no-hitter—Mets pitchers had won twenty games before, although not since Frank Viola did it in 1990. But it was close.

Bobby Parnell took the ball with one out in the ninth. He got Josh Harrison to bounce out.

One out to go.

The hitter was now José Tabata, the left fielder. On a 1-0 count, I heard the unmistakable *thwack* of wood making contact with leather. I was still just peeking, but I followed the movement of my teammates and knew Tabata had driven the ball to right, where Mike Baxter was on patrol. He had saved Johan's no-hitter with a spectacular catch earlier in the season. This time Mike didn't have to crash into anything to make the catch. He tracked the ball and locked it in his glove. The roar that went up was louder than anything I'd heard since we dropped out of the race, months before.

I had won twenty games. It was almost too much to take in. I could hardly believe I had done it.

I ran out of the dugout to thank Bobby for the save, to thank and hug everybody.

I finished the greatest season of my life with a record of 20-6, and a 2.73 ERA. I led the league in innings pitched (233⅔), strikeouts (230), complete games (5) and shutouts (3).

All that remained was to find out whether my performance would be worthy of a Cy Young Award from the Baseball Writers' Association of America. Gio Gonzalez of the Nationals had one more victory than I did. The Dodgers' Clayton Kershaw, the 2011 Cy Young winner, had a lower ERA. I was hearing all sorts of arguments and discussions by the media, dicing our stats every which way.

The award is not announced each year until after the World Series is over, but I made up my mind early on that I wasn't going to spend any time trying to evaluate my chances. I decided to just let it be. I'd love to win, because, well, who wouldn't want to win? It's the fulfillment of a dream I'd had since I played T-ball for Coach Teeter, the one who gave out yellow stars when you made a good play. But it's such a far-fetched dream—all the stars (not just the yellow ones) have to align for it to happen. I certainly never thought it would come true. Heck, I was really thrilled by the parking space.

The results were announced live on the MLB Network in the early evening of November 14. I was home in Nashville. A satellite TV truck was parked in our driveway, ready to record my reaction. We never thought to pencil the date of the Cy Young Award announcement onto the family calendar. Months earlier, Anne had made arrangements to spend the second week of November on vacation with some girlfriends, a much-needed break to recharge her batteries when the off-season arrived and I could be the full-time parent in charge.

The kids, my mom, Anne's mom and dad, and my agent and good friend, Bo McKinnis, gathered in the family room, in front of the big TV. Kate Hughes, a terrific young woman who helps Anne with the kids, was there too, holding up an iPod to the broadcast so that Anne could watch it on her iPod from the place where she was vacationing, which had a TV but no access to the MLB Network (imagine that).

I was sitting on a stool in my backyard with television floodlights set up next to the hutch where the kids' pet rabbits—Darth Vader, Princess Amidala, and their three bunnies—were probably wondering, along with my neighbors, just what the peanut butter was going on over at the Dickeys'.

When Jack O'Connell, secretary-treasurer of the BBWAA, walked across the studio set to a podium to make the announcement, he carried an envelope. Now I knew how actors feel on Oscar night. I tried to keep cool, but my heart was racing.

Jack began by talking about history being made tonight. "In fifty-six years of voting, no knuckleball pitcher has ever won a Cy Young, in either league," he said.

Thank you so much for that, Mr. O'Connell. That was an incredible blessing because before I even heard my name, I knew. I knew I had won the 2012 National League Cy Young Award. I had a moment to compose myself before Jack said, "Until now," and then read my name.

I will never have another moment like that one. I embraced it fully. I thought immediately about all the people who had loved me and believed in me, who made this moment possible. I thought again about the rocket-fueled power of hope.

A few seconds after I heard Jack declare me the winner in the earpiece I was wearing, there is another sound, *even sweeter,* if you can believe that.

There's a bit of a delay between the audio you hear if you're getting the feed directly from the satellite truck, and the moment it is broadcast through, say, your family TV.

The second sound I heard was ear-splitting joy, the sound of my kids, my family, my dear friends, erupting in celebration in the house behind me.

The noisemakers at Citi Field have nothing on the Dickey kids, folks.

I began the year on an African summit, and I ended it on a baseball summit. I like the symmetry. God is good.

INDEX